STUDIES IN CHURCH HISTORY

Vol. IV

Edited by

Matthew Spinka   Robert Hastings Nichols

Prize Essay
in the
FRANK S. BREWER FUND
Competition

CONGREGATIONALISM IN THE DUTCH NETHERLANDS

The Rise and Fall

of

The English Congregational Classis

1621-1635

By

RAYMOND PHINEAS STEARNS

Assistant Professor of History
The University of Illinois

▲ ▲ ▲

I appear'd before the arch-bishopp
And all the high Commission:
I gave no grace,
But told him to his face
That he favour'd superstition,
—*The Distracted Puritan,* by Dr. Richard Corbett.

THE AMERICAN SOCIETY OF CHURCH HISTORY
Chicago, Illinois
1940

Copyright, 1940, by
The American Society of Church History
Chicago, Ill.

PREFACE

This little book aims to set forth an account of the activities of an organized group of English Puritan refugees in the Dutch Netherlands roughly between the years 1621 and 1635. Most of the refugees belonged to that sect later known as Congregationalists, and this monograph treats of one of the earliest, possibly the first, successful attempts to practice the Congregational polity on an inter-church scale. Appended to the text are twenty documents or extracts from documents which illuminate the story of the Congregational classis and of the persons connected therewith. With one or two exceptions, as noted, none of these documents, to my knowledge, has been published before. They do more than merely enlarge upon the text. The story of the erection of the English church at Utrecht (Appendix V) might well serve as a prototype of all the English churches organized in the Netherlands; Thomas Hooker's answers to John Paget's "20 Propositions" (Appendix VIII) is one of the earliest expositions of the vital differences of opinion between Congregationalists and Presbyterians, foreshadowing later disputes of the English Civil Wars and many ecclesiastical problems of New England. I believe that both the text and the documents appended will be found of value to students of Puritanism in general and of Congregationalism in particular. They cast light also upon early New England history, Anglo-Dutch relations, and the English Merchant Adventurers in the Low Countries.

Parts of the following text were presented in my article, "The New England Way in Holland," in *The New England Quarterly* for December, 1933; the whole is an enlargement of a paper, "The English Congregational Classis in Holland, 1621-1635," which I read at the fourteenth spring meeting of the American Society of Church History in Indianapolis, Indiana, April 29, 1938. Except these brief treatments, only one of which is published, I know of no other account of the English Congregational classis in the Low Countries. Doubtless some contemporary writers knew something about it, and there are distorted hints concerning it in the works of English

Civil War polemical pamphleteers, notably in Thomas Edwards' *Gangraena*. More recent historians have little more. The Reverend William Steven was aware of the existence of the classis; D. Plooij, the late Dutch historian, was puzzled by it; and Champlin Burrage, though he probably knew much about it, found occasion to tell very little. Other historians of Puritanism appear unaware of the existence of the classis, of the hopes it engendered in Congregational breasts, of its effects upon English nonconformity, of its rôle in maturing Congregational polity, of its intimate connections with the founding of New England.

It is pleasant to recall by way of acknowledgment the assistance of numerous officials and attendants in several libraries from which materials for this study were collected. I wish to thank especially those of the British Museum, London, particularly of the Manuscripts Division; those of the Public Record Office, London; of Dr. Williams's Library, London; of the Royal Dutch Archives, The Hague; of the Library of the University of Leiden; of the Massachusetts Historical Society Library, Boston; and of Widener Library, Harvard University, Cambridge. I am indebted to my friend and colleague, Dr. Charles E. Odegaard, for a critical reading of the manuscript. The American Society of Church History has generously granted the proceeds of the Frank S. Brewer Fund for publication of this volume in the *Studies in Church History*. And, lastly, I wish to express appreciation and gratitude to my most helpful critic, copyist, typist, and wife, Elizabeth Scott Stearns.

R. P. S.

Urbana, Illinois
January, 1940

CONTENTS

INTRODUCTION

I.

The word "Puritan" is today an unfortunate term with a wide variety of meanings. Strangely enough, it has always been ambiguous, a name given to a number of ill-defined groups of men and women who wished to replace the ecclesiastical hierarchy of the sixteenth and seventeenth centuries by a new and purer "discipline out of the Word." Like Martin Luther, the early Puritans were looked upon by the prevailing civil and ecclesiastical authorities as dangerous and radical schismatics who blindly struggled to turn divinely constituted order into stupid, ungrounded chaos; yet by their professed efforts to re-institute early Christian practices in matters pertaining both to theology and ecclesiastical polity, by their repeated appeals to the works and reported systems of the Patristic writers, and by their stern rigidity in private deportment and social relationships they could, and often did, pose as true conservatives. Puritans were heirs of the Protestant Reformation. But they believed that reformation in England had not gone far enough, that the Elizabethan church settlement left many abuses yet to be corrected, that institutions still survived from the days of popery which should be eradicated, and that the Church of England should be restored to that "purity" which characterized the first century church as established by Christ Himself.

However, the distinctions between the Puritans and other contemporary Englishmen have often been over-emphasized. As Miller and Johnson have recently stated, if

. . . we wish to take Puritan culture as a whole, we shall find, let us say, that about ninety per cent of the intellectual life, scientific knowledge, morality, manners and customs, notions and prejudices, was that of all Englishmen. The other ten per cent, the relatively small number of ideas upon which there was dispute, made all the difference between the Puritan and his fellow-Englishmen. . . . [1]

Probably the root, or essence, of this difference—this crucial

---

1 Perry Miller and Thomas H. Johnson, *The Puritans* (*American Literature Series*, Harry Hayden Clark, General Editor. N. Y., 1938), 7.

1

"ten per cent"—lay in the Puritan belief that "Christ hath left us so perfect a rule and Discipline"[2] in the Bible that the Scriptures were, as the great William Perkins affirmed, "the only foundation of our faith and the rule and canon of all truth," comprehending "many holy sciences" as theology, ethics, economics, politics, ecclesiastical polity, and even psychology and education.[3] This belief, which Anglicans thought was too rigid, too doctrinaire, and an utterly unjustifiable extension of the authority of Scripture, in time came to be supplemented by another difference. As Tudor monarchy gave way to the divine right absolutism of the Stuarts, Anglicans came to defend the church settlement by appeals to royal prerogative while Puritans pinned their hopes for further reformation on Parliament. Thus to initial intellectual distinctions were added political differences which underlay the Civil Wars and the Glorious Revolution of seventeenth century England.

Thus far the term "Puritan" has been employed in a general sense. Nevertheless, though Puritans can be distinguished from Anglicans in a broad sense, as is demonstrated above, the word held a number of specific meanings as applied to a wide variety of dissenting sects—Presbyterians, Separatists, Congregationalists, Baptists, and even Fifth Monarchists, Quakers, and Diggers. For, while Puritans agreed that further church reformation was necessary and that "Christ hath left us a perfect rule and Discipline" in the Holy Scriptures, they wrangled as bitterly among themselves as with their enemies over the extent and degree of the reformation and the ultimate form which the "perfect rule and Discipline" was to take. Accordingly, as various students viewed the situation, casuistries became more and more refined until a Puritan appeared, as Samuel Butler wrote, one who

. . . could distinguish, and divide
A hair 'twixt south and south-west side.

The points of difference among Puritan sects were often small in present day eyes. But they were none the less bitter. Though the first English Civil War was fought between Round-

2 Walter Travers, *A full and plaine declaration of Ecclesiasticall Discipline out of the word of God* . . . (Leiden, 1617), 103. First published as *Ecclesiasticae disciplinae et Anglicanae Ecclesiae ab illa aberrationis plena e verbo Dei et dilucida explicatio*, in 1574.
3 Quoted in M. M. Knappen, *Tudor Puritanism* (Chicago, 1939), 355.

head and Cavalier, the second was between Congregationalist and Presbyterian; and Congregationalist and Presbyterian alike persecuted Quakers, Diggers, and Fifth Monarchists until the words of John Gauden in 1653 seem fully justified even for his day:

Little differences in Religion (like Crocodiles eggs) bring forth *prodigies;* which are ever growing greater till they dye; adding *fury* to faction; *passion* to opinion; *cruelty* to novelty; *Self-interests* to Conscience: *Divine vengeance* oft punishing sin with sin; extravagancies of judgements with exorbitancies of deeds; suffering the greater lust, or stronger faction (like pikes in a pond) to devoure the lesser; and one *error* to be both executioner and heir to another; . . . [4]

II.

It is with but one early phase in the history of one of these "prodigies" that the following little monograph deals. Yet no apology seems necessary for the limited scope in time and topic inasmuch as the enterprise described herein is perhaps the earliest experiment in Congregational polity on an inter-church scale and its failure, occasioned by no defects inherent in the system, closed one place of Puritan refuge to Congregationalists and forced the hand of that divine Providence which many of our Puritan forefathers claimed led them to the Massachusetts Bay Colony. The group of Puritans with which we are concerned would today be classified as Congregationalists and that is the term applied to them hereinafter. But during the early seventeenth century they were too imperfectly known to warrant a specific name. Contemporary writers often referred to them as "Jacobites" or "Amesians" because they adhered to a creed and polity which had evolved principally from the practices and teachings of Henry Jacob and Dr. William Ames. During the English Civil Wars they became known as Independents, though the term was sometimes loosely employed to include all the supporters of Oliver Cromwell, and English Independents, for political purposes, embraced principles of religious toleration which New England Congregationalists indignantly rejected. Present day historians, for purposes of accurate classification, often refer to this sect as "non-separating Congregationalists," for they neither denied that the

4 *Hieraspistes: A Defense by way of Apology for the Ministry and Ministers of the Church of England* (London, 1653), "To the Reader," unpaged.

Anglican church was a true church nor professed separation from it, as distinguished from their elder brothers, the Pilgrims, or "Brownists," who did.

This group of Puritans arose during the reign of James I. Neither their creed nor their polity was mature, however, until it was tempered by experience in the Low Countries, in the wilderness of the Massachusetts Bay, and on the battlefields of the English Civil Wars. Basically, their creed was Calvinism with some modifications and variations from that of the Presbyterians,[5] from whom they differed seriously, however, in matters pertaining to the constitution of the church. A church, according to Henry Jacob, "is a particular Congregation being a spirituall perfect Corporation of Believers & having power in it selfe immediately from Christ to administer all Religious meanes of faith to the members thereof."[6] Both Jacob and William Ames insisted that, according to the precedents of the primitive Christians, the churches are not "Diocesan Churches, but Particular Ordinary Congregations: and the Bishops, as they were peculiarly called after the Apostles, were only Parishional, not Diocesan, Bishops; differing from other Pastors only in priority of order, not in majority of rule."[7] A church, said Jacob, could be formed only "By a free Mutuall consent of Believers joyning & Covenanting to live as members of a holy Society together in all religious & vertuous duties as Christ & his Apostles did institute & practice in the Gospell."[8] Similarly, Ames asserted that "a congregation or particular Church is a society of believers joyned together by a speciall bond among themselves, for the constant exercise of the communion of Saints among themselves."[9] Membership is restricted to the proved "elect," and subscription to the "Covenant" is essential.[10] For, as Ames held,

5 Perry Miller has outlined these modifications and variations in ''The Marrow of Puritan Divinity,'' in *Publications* of the Colonial Society of Mass. (Boston, 1936), XXXII, 247-300.
6 See Jacob's Catechism in Champlin Burrage, *The Early English Dissenters in the Light of Recent Research* (2 vols., Cambridge, England, 1912), II, 157.
7 Jacob's ''Four Assertions'' in Benjamin Hanbury, *Historical Memorials Relating to the Independents, or Congregationalists* (3 vols., London, 1839), I, 222. See also William Ames, *The Marrow of Sacred Divinity* (London, 1642), Book I, 178-80.
8 Jacob's Catechism in Burrage, *English Dissenters.*
9 Ames, *The Marrow*, Book I, 139-40.
10 Miller, ''The Marrow of Puritan Divinity,'' in *Publications*, XXXII (1936), 258 ff.

Believers doe not make a particular Church, although peradventure many may meete and live together in the same place, unlesse they be joyned by a speciall bond among themselves: . . .

This bond is a covenant, either expresse or implicite, whereby believers doe particularly bind themselves to performe all those duties, both toward God and one toward another, which pertaine to the respect and edification of the Church.[11]

Each "particular Congregation" is "an entire and Independent body-politic," subject to no superior ecclesiastical authority. All the "particular Congregations" together constitute the Church Universal. Unity "standeth . . . upon the one Word & Testament of Christ," not upon "one Church or Pastor over the rest." Indeed, wrote Jacob to James I,

We acknowledge no other power and authority for the overseeing, ruling, and censuring of Particular Churches,—how many soever in number, —in the case of their misgovernment, than that which is originally invested in your Royal Person, and from it derived to such of your Laity, as you shall judge worthy to be deputed to the execution of the same under you. So as the favour humbly solicited, is, That whereas our Lord Jesus hath given to each Particular Church, or ordinary Congregation, this right and privilege, namely, to elect, ordain, and deprive her own Ministers; and, to exercise all the other parts of lawful ecclesiastical jurisdiction under Him, your Majesty would be pleased to order . . . That each Particular Church . . . may have, enjoy, and put in execution and practice this her said right and privilege. . . . Here we do humbly entreat that we may not be so interpreted as if we disclaimed all sorts of Synods. It is the Ruling, and not the Deliberative and Persuasive Synod, which we except against.[12]

In another instance Jacob wrote, "I affirme that no Synod under the Gospell hath power by Gods ordinance to prescribe & rule Ecclesiastically sundry whole Churches if they severally consent not."[13] However, congregations should enter into interchurch associations. Ames wrote:

Yet particular Churches, as their Communion doth require, the light of nature and equity of rules and examples of Scripture doe teach, may and oftentimes also ought to enter into a mutuall confederacy and fellowship among themselves in Classes and Synods, that they may use their common consent and mutuall helpe as much as fitly may be, in those things especially which are of greater moment; but that combination doth neither constitute a new forme of a Church, neither ought it to take away, or diminish any way, that liberty and power which Christ hath

11 Ames, *The Marrow*, Book I, 140-41.
12 Hanbury, *Memorials*, I, 225-26.
13 Burrage, *English Dissenters*, II, 165.

left to his Churches, for the directing and farthering whereof it only serves.[14]

Consistories, classes, synods, and other "consociations" of ministers and churches should be formed then, but they have no authority over particular congregations except to give them counsel and advice.[15]

This applied even to the calling and ordination of ministers. According to Congregational principles, a minister was lawfully minister only to his own church to which he had been formally called and in which he had been properly ordained. He was accounted minister by no other congregation; and without calling to and ordination in a particular church a man was no minister. "The Episcopall ordination of a Minister without title, that is without a Church to which and in which he should be ordained," wrote Ames, "is as ridiculous as if any should be fancied to be a husband without a wife."[16] The right of calling a minister belongs solely to the church to which he is to minister, "yet here they need the direction and helpe of the Elders, both of the same Church, and very often also of the neighbour Churches."[17] The essence of calling is election by the congregation and acceptance by the elected. Previous to the "call," the candidate is subject to examination and trial. And consummating the "call" is ordination, "which is nothing else than a certaine solemne entrance of the Minister already elected into the free execution of his function."[18] Thus a minister is created only by the particular church which he serves. He cannot forsake it without permission of his congregation, he cannot be a non-resident servant of his flock, and he cannot be ejected except by his own congregation—and that not without sufficient cause clearly demonstrable. His church is neither a civil nor a geographical unit, but a voluntary association of believers bound by a convenant. And though he and his congregation should associate with other churches in classes and synods, these classes and synods are not specific civil units or geographical areas and they have no lawful coercive authority

14 Ames, *The Marrow*, Book I, 179.
15 *See* Perry Miller, *Orthodoxy in Massachusetts* (Cambridge, 1933), Chapter IV, for an excellent analysis of Congregational polity.
16 Ames, *The Marrow*, Book I, 180.
17 *Ibid.*
18 Ames, *The Marrow*, Book I, 180.

over particular congregations except by way of persuasive
counsel and advice. According to Ames, the

transcendant members of the Hierarchy were meerly human Creatures
brought into the Church without any Divine precept or example: . . .
They rob the Churches of their liberty, whilst they exercise, as it were,
a regall, or rather tyrannicall, dominion over the Churches themselves,
and their Pastors; they have brought in with them the Roman Anti-
christ himselfe as the head, and Chancellors, Suffragenes, Arch-deacons,
Officials and the like props of the Hierarchy as the taile of the same
sort, (whose very names are Apocryphall and altogether unknowne to
the first Churches) to the utter oppressing of the Churches of God.[19]

Such, in broad outline, was the Congregational polity as set
forth by its founders. Its use of such terms as "the elect" and
"synod" often caused it to be mistaken for Presbyterianism;
and, indeed, Congregational retention of many Presbyterian
forms with denial of their substance was a source of constant
confusion and misunderstanding among Anglican, Presbyterian, and Dutch Reformed ecclesiastics.

The principles and practices of Congregationalism found
fullest expression first in the Dutch Netherlands. From the
time the Dutch states won their independence from Spain,
during Queen Elizabeth's reign, their tolerating practices in
matters of religion made them a desirable haven for English
ministers exiled for nonconformity. It was in Holland that
Henry Jacob, Robert Parker, William Ames, and other fathers
of Congregationalism first found that freedom from English
prelacy which enabled them to inaugurate and perfect their new
polity without effective opposition. By 1620, a score or more Congregational ministers and some of their flocks had found refuge,
toleration, and employment in Holland. As many—perhaps
most—of the English Congregationalists came from East
Anglian ports such as London, Boston, Norwich, and Great
Yarmouth, where they were engaged in the staple trade and
commercially connected with the Low Countries, it was no
unendurable hardship for them to transfer themselves and
their businesses to the flourishing Dutch marts. Others not
connected with the cloth trade could often find employment in
the rapidly expanding Dutch trade and commerce. No wonder,
then, when their plans to purge the Established Church of its
popish ceremonies failed in England and the archiepiscopal

19 *Ibid.*

reins began to tighten in the 1620's, the leaders of the sect, including both ministers and laymen, turned increasingly to the Dutch Netherlands for haven.   Only when this place of refuge was closed to them were they compelled to embark for the wildernesses of the New World.   The story of the closing of the Dutch Netherlands to non-separating Congregationalists is the story of the rise and fall of their classis in Holland.

CHAPTER I

FORMATION OF THE CLASSIS

I.

In the year 1621 eleven English and Scottish ministers, most of them exiled to the Dutch Netherlands for nonconformity to the Anglican church, petitioned James I of England for permission legally to establish a classis. Already, three years before, with His Majesty's approbation and with the sanction of Dutch civil and ecclesiastical authorities, they had formed a "Sinodale" association "for redresse of all enormities . . . in deportinge or putting away of some scandalous parsons and entertayninge and putting in their places persons more fitt and in our uniformity . . . with the churches where we Live and the good contentment of our superiors under whome wee exercyse our places."[1] Now, "being againe assembled to the same happy intents and having had notice by your Majestys Ambassader [Sir Dudley Carleton] of your Majestys pleasure to sett over us a Moderator to be appointed by your Majesty," they hoped to escape "the Inconveniences and Impossibilities"[2] of such a meddlesome and embarrassing course and prayed the king not only "To graunte and consente That wee maye goe forward and prosper withoute any hinder or Interruption," but also requested His Majesty's approval of an English classis like those already existing among the French and Walloon churches in the Low Countries.

The petitioners took care to emphasize that ample precedent for such an ecclesiastical organization existed in the practices of other foreign groups in Holland and that, "for the removall of all jealousies of innovation, separation, faction, or schisme" the "Most Illustrious Lords" of the Dutch States General approved their design.[3] And they were at equal pains to avoid

---

1 "Boswell Papers," *Add. MSS* 6394, I, fols. 18-21. In the British Museum. Hereinafter cited as *Boswell Papers*. This document is printed in full in Appendix I.
2 These are verbosely enumerated in *ibid*.
3 *Boswell Papers*, I, fol. 17. Printed in Appendix II.

the appearance of rupture with the Church of England, as they protested themselves to be

. . . free in their soules and consciences from any disrespect, censure, prejudice, or condemnation of the churches of his Majesties dominions, reserving unto them all due reverence and acknowledgment as to the true Churches of Christ, equally precious in the sight of God (through the same most precious faith) with our selves; resolving still to hold communion with them notwithstanding any difference of externall order; . . . [4]

James I viewed the petition with favor and granted the ministers permission to organize a classis after the pattern of the French and Dutch Reformed churches in order that they might have an agency "to suppresse those who took upon them the function of preachers without Lawful vocation or Admission to the Ministry. And 2ly. to examine, restraine, and punish the ill manners of such as give scandall by their vitious lives."[5] Moreover, the classis was to suppress books and pamphlets "any way derogatory to the Church or State of England." That James should intend ministers who had been exiled for nonconformity to effect a "classical" organization abroad and through it support English prelacy is humorous indeed; but such appear to have been his anticipations, and the petitioners' protestations of ostensible conformity lent color to his intentions. The hairsplitting tenets of non-separating Congregationalists were not yet comprehended in English ecclesiastical circles.

It was simple enough for the ministers to effect an organization somewhat like the Dutch. But they were unwilling to join the Dutch classes, and Congregational principles forbade them to admit their authority. Accordingly, they sought the approval of the South Holland Synod and, with its advice, petitioned the Dutch States General for permission to organize a classis of English and Scottish ministers independent of Dutch ecclesiastical establishments.[6] After some deliberations

4 *Ibid.*
5 *Boswell Papers*, I, fols. 40-44. Printed in Appendix VI. See also *Calendar of State Papers, Domestic Series, Charles I, 1629-1631*, 110.
6 *Boswell Papers*, I, fols. 22-23. Printed in Appendix III. The specific petition to the States General has not been found. But it was debated by the Council of State and reported to the States General on Sept. 11, 1621, as is shown in the *Archief van de Staten-Generaal*: ''Registers van ordinaris Resolutien,'' No. 570 (1621), fol. 437 b (The Hague, Holland). At this time the States General were disposed in favor of the proposed classis in order to stop ''schandalouse onordeninge'' in the English and Scottish churches. But they withheld action until they had seen a list of the ministers petitioning.

with the Council of State and with the English Ambassador, the Dutch authorities approved the creation of "the Synod of the English and Scottish Ministers in the Netherlands" for the purpose of "the better ordering" of the said ministers in their midst according to the examples set by the French and Walloon churches.[7] Thus, by means of the grant of James I and the commission of the Dutch government, the ministers were legally at liberty to erect their own ecclesiastical structure practically free from all outside interference.

To be sure, they had not gained this ecclesiastical freedom without guile. James and the English Privy Council doubtless thought that they intended a Presbyterian synod which would be under the authority of, or closely checked by, the Dutch Reformed Church; and the English authorities, with an eye to problems in conformity created by Dutch, French, and Walloon churches in London and vicinity, had consented to the classis, in part at least, as a handsome but not disinterested gesture to the Dutch nation. Similarly, the Dutch officials, led on by the French and Walloon precedents and with no notion that the English and Scottish classis would be organized upon a basis vastly different from their own synods, granted it an existence separate from the Dutch ecclesiastical system as a friendly gesture to the petitioners' nationalities. Perhaps the end justified the means. In any case, Congregational ministers, as events showed, came to look upon the classis in Holland as a license for practice in the Dutch Netherlands of "Discipline out of the Word" as seen through Congregational eyes. The self-styled saints who erected the classis in 1621 must have congratulated themselves as others of their number did when, nearly a decade later, they slipped out of England with the charter of the Massachusetts Bay Company in their possession.

II.

That there was a sufficient number of Congregational ministers regularly employed in the Dutch Netherlands to form

7 *Archief van de Staten-Generaal*: "Registers van ordinaris Resolutien," No. 570 (1621), fol. 503 b (The Hague); William Steven, *The History of the Scottish Church, Rotterdam* (Edinburgh and Rotterdam, 1833), 261-65, 397; *Boswell Papers*, I, fols. 22-23, 146.

and maintain the English classis is explained by a glance at Anglo-Dutch relations during the previous hundred and fifty years or so. Two large groups of English and Scottish people had settled in the Dutch Netherlands among whom English ministers exiled for nonconformity had, since the days of the Marian exiles, found little difficulty in obtaining employment. The more important of the two was the English Merchant Adventurers who had been chartered since the fifteenth century to manage the great staple trade between England and the Low Countries.[8] The second group consisted of several regiments of English and Scottish soldiers sent to the Dutch states in the 1580's to assist the Dutch in maintaining their newly declared independence from Spain. These troops were renewed from time to time and, in the 1620's, the English soldiers of the "four standing Colonels in the Low Countries" consisted of some sixty-eight companies.[9] Thus, before the end of the sixteenth century, almost every major town in the Dutch Netherlands contained a group of English people—merchant adventurers, soldiers in garrison, and religious refugees. Frequently these groups combined—generally with Dutch finan-

8 E. M. Carus-Wilson, "The Origins and Early Development of the Merchant Adventurers' Organization in London as Shown in Their Own Mediaeval Records," *The Economic History Review*, IV (April, 1932), 146-76; W. E. Lingelbach, "The Merchant Adventurers of England," in *Translations and Reprints from the Original Sources of European History*, 2nd Series, II (Philadelphia, 1920), 189-90; R. Bijlsma, *Rotterdams Welvaren, 1550-1650* (The Hague, 1918), 142 ff.

9 J. A. Froude, *History of England* (12 vols., London, 1870-72), XII, 1 ff; P. J. Blok, *History of the People of the Netherlands* (4 vols., N. Y., 1907), IV, 13. For materials relating to these regiments, *see*: Clements R. Markham, *The Fighting Veres* (Boston, 1888), 397 and *passim*; Rev. Alexander B. Grosart (ed.), *The Voyage to Cadiz in 1625, Being a Journal Written by John Glanville (Camden Society Publications*, n.s., XXXII, Westminster, 1883), 3; George W. Johnson, *The Fairfax Correspondence* (2 vols., London, 1848), *passim*; and *Memoires De Frederic Henri De Naussau, Prince D'Orange . . . Depuis 1621 jusqu'au 1646* (Amsterdam, 1733), 51-121, 131-43. Chief among the English regiments were those of Sir Horatio (Colonel) Vere whose chaplain, in 1611, was William Ames [Edmund Sawyer, (ed.), *Memorials of . . . Sir Ralph Winwood* (3 vols., London, 1725), III, 346-47] and whose wife was a friendly correspondent of John Davenport [*Proceedings* of the Mass. Hist. Society, XLII, 207-10]; Sir Edward (Colonel) Harwood, a very religious man, puritanically inclined [*Dict. Nat. Biog.*]; and Col. Charles Morgan, who patronized Congregational chaplains almost exclusively [Sir William Dugdale, *A Short View of the Late Troubles* (Oxford, 1681), 32; *Boswell Papers*, I, fols. 84, 91, 126, 134, 140, 152]. Scottish regiments also aided the Dutch in the 1620's [James Ferguson (ed.), *Papers Illustrating the History of the Scots Brigade in the Service of the United Netherlands, 1572-1782*, in *Publications of the Scottish History Society*, XXXII (2 vols., Edinburgh, 1899), I, 310-12].

cial assistance—to form a church and employ a minister.[10] By
the 1620's English congregations had been organized at Amsterdam, Leiden, Campvere, Flushing, Delft, Utrecht, Dort,
Middelburgh, The Hague, Rotterdam, and possibly elsewhere.
Each of these had a building in which to conduct religious
services and a settled minister; and, in addition to these, more
than a dozen English and Scottish chaplains served the garrisons or regiments in the field.[11]

These English and Scottish congregations were Puritan
almost without exception. A few were Separatists of the
Brownist or Barrowist varieties,[12] some were Scottish (or
English) Presbyterians,[13] and some conformed to the Dutch
Reformed Church and were members of Dutch synods;[14] but
a considerable number were Congregationalists. Their ministers—excepting those who had joined Dutch synods—were
free to practise Puritan ways as they saw fit. Neither the
English church nor the Dutch exercised formal ecclesiastical
supervision over the army chaplains except in so far as the
latter may have been able to draw them into Dutch synods
through control over the chaplains' salaries.[15] The ministers
to the Merchant Adventurers were equally free from ecclesiastical oversight. The English society of Merchant Adventurers
was controlled by a court consisting of a governor and assistants
chosen by the members in the Low Countries. This court,

10 *See*, for example, ''A true Relation of the first Erection of an English Church
   in Utrecht. With the proceedings since,'' in *Boswell Papers*, I, fols. 270-75.
   Printed in Appendix V.
11 ''English Preachers in the Netherlands,'' *Boswell Papers*, I, fol. 175. Printed
   in Appendix IV. See also David Masson, *The Life of John Milton* (6 vols.,
   London and N. Y., 1859-80), I, 317-18; Daniel Neal, *The History of the
   Puritans* (2 vols., N. Y., 1871), I, 242 ff.
12 John Robinson and Hugh Goodyear, of Leiden, for instance.
13 Mr. ''Duglasse'' [Douglas?] of Col. Ogle's regiment, and possibly Drake of
   Middelburgh.
14 John Paget of Amsterdam, Fortree of Utrecht, and Gribbins of ''Busch''
   [Bois-le-Duc].
15 Sir Dudley Carleton, when questioned on the point of English supervision, wrote
   (April 25, 1637): ''the matter in question was never urged nor pressed; but
   the governors of the Church of England connived at it, for aught I know . . .
   The [Dutch] States ever carryed themselves indifferently in business of this
   nature and left the forme of the service to the discretion of the minister.
   But in the first treaty when the Earle of Leicester came into the Country, about
   '84 or '85 was an article expressly capitulating the use of the established public
   forme of God's service in the Church of England, . . . And without question
   that was the beginning of all English Churches in the Low Countreys;
   however they fell from it afterwards.''—Carleton to Boswell, in *Boswell Papers*,
   I, fols. 257-58.

according to the charter, had full authority to make laws and ordinances for the society and "to ende and determine all civill causes, questions, and controversies arising between or among the brethren" without appeal.[16] The latest charter, granted in 1564, made no specific provision for ecclesiastical establishments. Churches were simply organized by the merchants themselves as needs arose—usually with Dutch financial assistance. Their ministers, then, had no civil or ecclesiastical superiors except the local deputies appointed by the governor and assistants of the company. The ministers of the Congregationalist persuasion, then, had been free, negatively speaking, to erect a classis without appeal to English or Dutch authorities; the official sanctions of the two states merely gave them positive authority to act without danger of civil or ecclesiastical interference.

Evidently the leader among the Congregational ministers who founded the English classis was John Forbes who lately (1621) had become minister to the church of the Merchant Adventurers at Delft. Middle-aged, well-educated, and widely experienced, Forbes had once been a popular and distinguished Scottish Presbyterian minister and moderator (1606) of the Aberdeen Assembly.[17] But running afoul of the English Privy Council, whose spiritual authority he declined to honor, he was imprisoned, tried for high treason, and banished from the kingdom. He left England (November, 1606), travelled widely on the Continent, and finally settled (1611) as minister to the English Merchant Adventurers at Middelburgh where he served for a decade. While at Middelburgh, Forbes's experiences and associates inclined him towards Congregationalism. Perhaps it was Henry Jacob himself who turned Forbes to these views, as the two men were colleagues at Middelburgh for a time between 1611 and 1621. But whatever effected his shift in allegiance, it is clear that by 1621 Forbes was a Congregationalist.[18]

16 Lingelbach, "The Merchant Adventurers," xvi, 5; also Lingelbach, "The Internal Organization of the Merchant Adventurers of England," in *Transactions of the Royal Historical Society*, n.s., XVI (London, 1901), 19-67. The court met on the Continent: at Antwerp, until its sack by the Duke of Alva; in 1587 it was moved to Middelburgh whence, in 1621, it was transferred to Hamburg.

17 *Dictionary of National Biography*; George Roberts (ed.), *Diary of Walter Yonge, Esq.* (London: Camden Society, 1848), 11.

18 Champlin Burrage, *The English Dissenters*, I, 296-300; Steven, *Scottish Church*, 294-97.

Associated with John Forbes at the founding of the classis were John Wing and John Hassall, ministers at The Hague; Thomas Scott, soon (1622) to become "the first Minister of this settled Congregation" at Utrecht;[19] Thomas Barkeley, minister at Rotterdam; Samuel Bachelor, a Puritan pluralist who was both minister at Gorinchem and "Preacher to the Regiment of Sir Charles Morgan Knight and Colonel;" and Walter Whetstone, Andrew Hunter, George Clarke, Alexander Clarke, and John Oswald—all chaplains to English or Scottish troops in the Low Countries.[20] Within the next decade or so the classis added to its roll of members a Mr. Paine, of Bergen-op-Zoom; Mr. Sibbald, of Nimwegen; Mr. Widdow, of Husden; Mr. Roe, of Flushing; Mr. Balmford, of The Hague; Thomas Hooker, later of Connecticut fame, who became assistant to Forbes at Delft from 1630 to 1633; Hugh Peter, later of Salem, Massachusetts, and stormy petrel of the English Civil Wars, who succeeded Barkeley at Rotterdam about 1630; and John Davenport, later of New Haven, Connecticut, who, by his efforts to become assistant to John Paget at Amsterdam in 1633 and later, stirred up a mighty rumpus which contributed to the enforced dissolution of the classis. Lastly, as sympathetic friend, influential adviser, and member in his last years, the classis had Dr. William Ames. Well known and highly respected in Puritan circles, Ames had been fellow of Christ's College, Cambridge, but was forced into exile for nonconformity in 1610. He preached among the English in Holland for several years, took part in the famous Synod of Dort in 1618, became professor of theology at the Friesland University of Franeker in 1622 and rector of the university from 1626 until he retired in 1633 to preach with Hugh Peter in Rotterdam and help found a proposed Congregational college for that community.[21] There he died late in 1633. Next to John Cotton, the early Congregationalists had no more able and scholarly defender than William Ames. His association with the English classis gave it prestige which it

---

19 *Boswell Papers*, I, fols. 270-75. Printed in Appendix V.
20 See *Boswell Papers*, I, fols. 17 (Appendix II), 175 (Appendix IV). Some of these can be identified more exactly: Whetstone was "preacher to the Regiment of Viscount Lisle"; and one of the Clarkes (Alexander?) was "the Scotch regiment Preacher to the Earle of Bucklough."
21 Hugo Visscher, *Guilielmus Amesius. Zijn Leven en Werken* (Haarlem, 1894), *passim; Dictionary of National Biography.*

could never have possessed without him.   Such was the membership of the English classis.

It was a roll, however, equally significant for its omissions. For example, John Paget, the Presbyterian watchdog of the English Church in Amsterdam; Thomas Potts, co-pastor with Paget; Isaac Fortree, of Utrecht; and one or two others positively refused to join the English classis and associated themselves instead with the Dutch synods in their respective communities.   Moreover, a few English chaplains—Stephen Goffe, for instance—conformed to the Anglican church and refused to adhere either to the English or the Dutch ecclesiastical organizations in Holland.   And Hugh Goodyear of Leiden and a few other contrary souls refused all these polities and went their own solitary, Separatist ways.[22]   These omissions caused considerable concern in Dutch official circles, for the Dutch authorities had intended the English classis to embrace all the English and Scottish ministers in their midst and to reduce them to an orderly ecclesiastical life with responsible oversight. By its failure to be all-inclusive, the classis fell short of one of the objects for which the Dutch had commissioned it. Furthermore, attempts by leaders of the classis to enlarge the membership or to exercise control over non-members among their English and Scottish brethren in Holland led to bitter clashes between the Congregationalists of the classis, on the one hand, and Anglicans, Presbyterians, and Separatists on the other.[23]   As both sides often appealed to Dutch authorities for support, the latter became increasingly aware of the fact that the classis occasionally multiplied among the English and Scottish ministers some of the distressful disorders which it had been designed (as the Dutch understood it) to eradicate. Nevertheless, the Dutch were tolerant of these difficulties and, as the classis functioned smoothly among its members, no official action was taken against it.   Only after the lapse of more than a decade, when English officials found cause to object to acts of the Congregational classis in Holland, were these original

---

22 *Boswell Papers*, I, fol. 175 (Appendix IV); Burrage, *English Dissenters*, II, 267-78.

23 For example, the classis attempted to prevent members and non-members from using the English prayer book [See *Boswell Papers*, I, fols. 172, 107 (Appendix XV), 152 (Appendix XVII)]; and it tried to force Paget and Potts of Amsterdam—already members of the Dutch Synod—into the English classis [See *ibid.*, I, fol. 146 (Appendix IX)].

shortcomings emphasized in order to arouse Dutch authorities to disciplinary action. Meanwhile, the members of the English classis conducted one of the earliest experiments in Congregational polity.

CHAPTER II

REVERBERATIONS IN ENGLAND

I.

Puritan ministers in exile were in constant communication with their fellow nonconformists in the homeland. Sympathetic merchants, sailors, and travellers carried clandestine letters and other papers which, despite the vigilance of English authorities, kept Puritans on both sides of the English Channel mutually well informed of what was going on. Nor is it surprising that this should have been the case. They had a common holy cause in "church reformation." Moreover, most of the ministers in exile were eager, if opportunity offered, to return to their former livings and they watchfully observed the course of events in England, sighing for the long awaited "reformation" or a toleration, howsoever tenuous, that would permit reunion with their old friends. Conversely, nonconformists in England, kept constantly on the anxious seat during these early Stuart days, not only sympathized with their brethren overseas but also, through them, kept open a weather eye for ministerial positions lest they or their godly friends suddenly find it expedient or necessary to seek refuge abroad for themselves.

The course of nonconformity grew increasingly difficult in England during the decade of the 1620's. Though James I, years before at the Hampton Court Conference, had made clear his position regarding Puritans, enforcement of that position rested largely upon ecclesiastical officials; and when Dr. George Abbot succeeded Archbishop Bancroft in 1610, the latter part of James's reign became as notable for laxity toward Puritans as the early part had been for severity.[1] But all this changed in the 1620's. King James was succeeded by Charles I in 1625 and the latter's sincere Anglicanism together with his high-spirited, ominously "popish," French bride and a predilection for such favorites as Buckingham and grim little William Laud did not augur well for the future of English

1 Peter Heylin, *Cyprianus Anglicus* (London, 1671), 57-59; 161, 190.

Puritanism. Laud was elevated to the diocese of Bath and Wells in 1626, to the Privy Council in 1627. When Archbishop Abbot showed too much lenity towards nonconformists, the King temporarily placed the archbishopric in the hands of a commission composed of Bishops Mountain, Neile, Buckeridge, Howson, and Laud.[2] Five years later, in 1633, William Laud was made Archbishop of Canterbury. In the meantime, while the Congregational classis in Holland grew in numbers and experience, many of the most carefully laid plans of the English Congregationalists were frustrated.

Two of these plans demand elucidation. Their failure, at a time of increasing prelatical vigilance in England, affected the Congregational classis in Holland by driving into Dutch exile prominent Puritan ministers who, by associating themselves with the classis, drew the watchful eyes of Laud to it. Both of the schemes stemmed from Archbishop Abbot's time, that "favourer" of Puritans under whose aegis non-conforming lecturers multiplied and Congregationalism grew in strength. The first was merely a revival of an early Puritan tactic to which Congregationalists, with other breeds of nonconformists, adhered. Since Tudor times, Puritans, finding the Crown adamant to their demands for ecclesiastical reforms, had turned to Parliament where a few puritanically inclined members either by themselves or—as was more often the case —in alliance with lawyers, Erastians, or other "political Puritans," might advance "church reformation" or ameliorate the lot of nonconforming clergymen by legislative means.[3] The early years of Charles's reign appeared to promise fruitful returns from this source. Not only were Puritans stronger in numbers both in and out of Parliament, but Protestants everywhere were dismayed by the Stuarts' paltry efforts on behalf of the Palatinate Germans and alarmed at Charles's pro-French foreign policy and pro-Catholic ecclesiastical intentions at home. The spread of Arminianism and "popery" in England aroused true Anglicans as well as Puritans. The Queen was a papist; the King was trying to relax the laws against recusants; and William Laud, though he vigorously denied it, was widely accounted an Arminian. Moreover, the King needed money badly—was reduced, in fact, to unconstitutional means of rais-

2 Oct. 9, 1627, *see ibid.,* 161.
3 M. M. Knappen, *Tudor Puritanism,* 265 ff.

ing it; and had awakened the opposition of lawyers and others jealous of the "ancient rights and liberties of Englishmen." To Puritans the time appeared ripe for a legislative *quid pro quo.* Parading under an honest political banner designed to eradicate popery and Arminianism and to check the King's exercise of unconstitutional prerogatives, Puritans could climb upon the political bandwagon with Anglicans, lawyers, Erastians, and others, exact concessions from Charles in return for parliamentary grants of funds and, in turn, gain from their erstwhile political allies some legislative crumbs in the way of "purifying" the Established Church after a fashion dear to the hearts of nonconformists.[4]

But Puritan and parliamentarian alike failed to reckon with the new King's resourcefulness in exercise of his prerogative. Charles's first and second parliaments, assembled in the first two years of his reign, were dissolved with no results except to heighten suspicions regarding his policies and his ministers.[5]   Naturally, the third parliament, called in 1628, was even less tractable and, after listing grievances against the King, resolving that consideration of grievances must precede supplies, and forcing Charles to accede to the Petition of Right, the Parliament was dissolved and the King determined never to call another unless he felt certain that it would do his pleasure.[6] With Sir John Eliot and others in prison as martyrs to the parliamentary cause against royal prerogative, and with a few resolutions passed against papists and Arminians, Charles's third parliament disbanded (March, 1629). Eleven years passed before a Parliament was summoned again. During this time, Puritan hopes to "purify" the Anglican church or to ameliorate the condition of nonconformists by parliamentary action were necessarily in abeyance. Not until the "Personal Rule" of Charles I ended with the calling of the "Short Parliament" in 1640 were these hopes revived.

The second plan was largely, if not solely, a Congregationalist scheme and, whether for that reason or not, it was

4 Godfrey Davies, *The Early Stuarts, 1603-1660* (Oxford, England, 1937), 42ff.
5 Samuel Rawson Gardiner (ed.), *The Constitutional Documents of the Puritan Revolution* (3d ed., Oxford, England, 1906), 1-64.
6 Gardiner, *Documents*, 65 ff.   Appropriate volumes in S. R. Gardiner, *History of England from the Accession of James I to the Outbreak of the Civil War 1603-1642* (new ed., 10 vols., London, 1890), supply a mass of factual data. *See* especially VI, 1-166.

more subtle. By endowment of organized feoffees to purchase lay impropriations, advowsons, and presentations, Congregationalists, working within the framework of the Established Church, would gradually acquire livings from which they could eject orthodox Anglicans and install "godly, able, and orthodox Ministers" in their stead.[7] The plan started about 1612 but for lack of funds nearly collapsed, and from 1617 to 1626 it was kept alive chiefly by the efforts of Richard Stock, rector of Allhallows, Bread Street, London.[8] Early in 1626, however, new life was injected into the scheme by the organization of twelve feoffees to manage the business, "four divines to persuade men's consciences,[9] four lawyers to draw all conveyances,[10] and four citizens who commanded rich coffers,[11] wanting nothing save what since doeth all things—some swordsmen to defend all the rest."[12] These men, with "sundry Agents, and Messengers whom they imployed about that business,"[13] collected money and gifts with which they purchased lay impropriations, took the advowsons and presentations into their own hands, and introduced new ministers of Congregational persuasions.[14] Thus, by boring quietly from within, they would have strengthened Congregationalism at the expense of the English church and as they understood it, furthered "the glorious Reformation" in England.

One of the most effective projects of the feoffees was conducted by a sub-committee called the "Collectors of St.

7 Samuel Clarke, *A Collection of the Lives of Ten Eminent Divines* (London, 1662), 110-11.
8 Frances Rose-Troup, *John White* (N. Y. and London, 1930), 247-48; Henry A. Parker, "The Feoffees of Impropriations," *Transactions* of the Colonial Society of Mass., XI (Boston, 1910), 263-77.
9 Dr. William Gouge of Blackfriars, London; Dr. Richard Sibbes, Master of Katherine Hall, Cambridge; Dr. Charles Offspring; and John Davenport, then of the Coleman Street Church, London.
10 Robert Eyre and Samuel Brown of Lincoln's Inn; Christopher Sherland and John White of Gray's Inn.
11 John Geering, grocer; Richard Davis, vintner; Francis Bridges, salter; and George Harwood, haberdasher and brother of the Colonel Harwood in the Low Countries. Rose-Troup, *John White*, 248-49, gives brief sketches of all these men.
12 Thomas Fuller, *The Church History of Britain* (3d ed., 3 vols., London, 1842), III, 362. Later a thirteenth feoffee, Alderman Rowland Heylin, was added to allow the casting of a vote. See Rose-Troup, *John White*, 248.
13 Clarke, *Lives*, 110.
14 For examples, *see Calendar of State Papers, Dom. Series, Charles I, 1633-34*, 192-93, 287. Laud wrote in 1633 that the feoffees "were the main Instruments for the *Puritan* Faction to undo the Church"; Henry Wharton (ed.), *The History of the Troubles and Tryall of . . . William Laud* (London, 1695), 47.

Antholin's." The church of St. Antholin's was a noted Puritan resort in Budge Row, London. During Queen Elizabeth's reign, six weekly lectures in divinity had been established there. By sly purchases, these foundations fell into the hands of the feoffees.[15] They appointed to the charges young Puritan lecturers and St. Antholin's soon became known as a Puritan seminary which, according to a later Royalist view, sent out "most of the Seditious Preachers" of the kingdom "to poyson the People with their Antimonarchical Principles."[16]

For several years after the reorganization in 1626 the feoffees prospered in their efforts. Considerable funds were collected, some thirteen impropriations had been purchased, the incomes of several worthy ministers in poor parishes had been augmented, and the widows and orphans of others had been protected. But the glorious work came to an ignominious end in 1633 when Laud, now Archbishop of Canterbury, having his attention directed to the feoffees by Peter Heylin,[17] prompted Attorney General Noy to investigate. As a result, the Attorney General called the feoffees into the Court of the Exchequer, demanded an account of what money had been collected and how it had been used, and, after considerable debate, ordered them (February 13, 1632/33) to hold no more assemblies and to deal no more in impropriations and advowsons; for, as the court held, they had usurped the "King's Regality" by assuming the power to form a corporate body and they had employed that power in a manner considered dangerous both to the church and state of England.[18] The feoffees were dissolved, the fruits of their labors were confiscated by the Crown, and the second Congregational plan was blasted.[19]

---

15 Rose-Troup, *John White*, 253-54; Fuller, *Church History*, III, 371-72.
16 Sir William Dugdale, *A Short View of the Late Troubles* (Oxford, 1681), 37.
17 Heylin, *Cyprianus*, 198-200; J. P. Lawson, *The Life and Times of William Laud* (2 vols., London, 1829), I, 551-52.
18 John Rushworth, *Historical Collections* (7 vols., London, 1659-1701), II, 150-52; Wharton, *William Laud*, 47; *Cal. of State Papers, Dom. Ser., Chas. I, 1633-34,* 192-93.
19 During the trial of the feoffees, while Laud jotted down prayers of thanksgiving in his diary, John Davenport, one of the feoffees involved, who soon afterwards sought refuge among his colleagues in Holland, wrote of that curiously cautious proposition which he made to God: that if He "be pleased to grant, that they might get no advantage against us, to punish us as *evil doers;* promising to observe what *answer* he gave, Which seeing he hath graciously done, and delivered me *from the thing I feared,* I record to these ends: 1. To be more *industrious* in my *family.* 2. To check my unthankfulness. 3. To quicken my self to

II.

The elevation of William Laud to high positions of ecclesiastical authority in the early reign of Charles I and the simultaneous destruction of Congregationalist hopes and plans for church "reformation" in England left nonconforming Congregationalists no recourse but reluctantly to seek refuge abroad. However, like the Separatists before them, it was the Dutch Netherlands towards which they first turned their eyes. The Massachusetts Bay Colony was as yet only a dream haven, far distant, uncertain, expensive, and dangerous. Holland, on the other hand, was near, willing to receive English refugees, and able to employ their labors. Congregational exiles already had settled there in considerable numbers and the successful establishment of their classis, legally independent of English and Dutch ecclesiastical authorities, made the Dutch Netherlands appear to be the most attractive place of refuge to hard-pressed Congregationalists in England. Accordingly, in the late 1620's and early 1630's, as Laud's systematic extirpation of all nonconformists got under way in England, such men as Hugh Peter, Thomas Hooker, and John Davenport joined Forbes, Ames, and other victims of earlier archiepiscopal wrath in Holland.

The existence of their independent classis in Holland undoubtedly added to the attractions of the Dutch Netherlands as a place of refuge for English Congregationalists. However, just as the course of nonconformity became rough in England in the late 1620's, so had that of the classis, despite its guarantees from the King of England and from the Dutch States General. Shortly after Charles I became king, it was noised about in the English Privy Council that John Forbes and the Congregational classis had assumed power to ordain ministers, had introduced a new liturgy in their churches, and had done other things contrary to the intent of the royal grants of 1618 and 1621. Sir Dudley Carleton, lately made Lord Carleton of Imbercourt and soon to be created Viscount Dorchester, a

thankfulness. 4. To awaken my self to more *watchfulness* for the time to come, in remembrance of his mercy. Which I beseech the Lord to grant; upon whose *faithfulness* in *his Covenant,* I cast myself, to be made *faithful* in *my Covenant."* See Cotton Mather, *Magnalia Christi Americana* (2 vols., Hartford, 1820), I, 294. Laud recorded that "The Criminal Part [was] reserved." Wharton, *William Laud,* 47.

member of the Privy Council and ambassador to The Hague, investigated these reports and placed his findings before the Privy Council in April, 1628. They issued "articles," May 19/29, which Lord Carleton passed on to the classis. The Council instructed that:[20]

. . . It is his Majesties pleasure that the said Ministers meddle not with the making or composing, much less the publishing of any new Liturgie or sett forme of prayer for their congregations.

. . . That they by no meanes do exercise the power of Ordination; but that they leave both English & Scottish to receive holy orders only from their owne mother-churches established in those two kingdomes: And that they accept of no other into any pastorall charge, but those only who have beene so ordained.

That they bring in no novelties in any rites or Ceremonies. . . .

. . . That they assume no power to themselves to meddle with any point of doctrine. . . .

"His Majestie is well content," the articles concluded, "that they should still keepe that power [of the classis] which King James his Royall Father intended to them," but the ministers were cautioned

In case any doubt or difficulty arise concerning the true meaning or execution of these particulars, that they then repaire to his Majesties Ambassador or Agent for the time being who will ever have or be able to procure such directions from his Majesty whereby so godly a worke may be duely & rightly advanced.

The Congregational classis, assembled at Rotterdam, sent a lengthy reply to these articles on June 4, 1628.[21] It began by beseeching

. . . your Royall Majestie to consider how unjustly, without any occasion by us ministers to these Churches of England & Scotland, a needless trouble hath beene raised unto us . . . upon some sinister suggestions only, as though our proceedings in our Synodall Assemblies should be derogatory to the Churches of the said kingdomes; whereas that solemne protestation made by us to the contrary att our first embracing & undertaking that authority given us by the most Illustrious Lords the States Generall by the procurement of his Majesties Ambassador doth sufficiently cleare us of that imputation.

20 *Boswell Papers,* I, fols. 40-44. Printed in Appendix VI. Carleton was careful that the Dutch authorities be informed of these articles and the States General received a copy on July 12. See *Archief van de Staten-Generaal*: ''Registers der brieven Memorien en bijlagen ingekomen uit Engeland,'' No. 4281 (1626-30), fols. 189-90 (The Hague). Also ''Registers van Ordinaris Resolutien,'' No. 577, fols. 360-61.

21 The reply appears in *Boswell Papers,* I, fols. 40-44. Printed in Appendix VI. This, too, Carleton communicated to the States General on July 12. See *Archief van de Staten-Generaal*: ''Registers von Ordinaris Resolutien'' (1621), No. 570, fols. 190-98. Also *ibid.*, No. 577, fols. 361 b - 364.

A verbatim copy of the protestation made in 1621[22] followed after which the ministers' tone hardened:

. . . we humbly beseech your Majestie to take notice of the most wise, religious, & just resolution of your Majesties father of happy memory, not only practised but also published by him; not to meddle with any but those within the precincts of his own dominions, & to leave it absolutely free to every Christian King, Prince, & Commonwealth to prescribe unto theirs the enternall forme of Ecclesiasticall government, which godly pattern if it shall please your Majestie to follow on our behalfe (who although by birth we acknowledge our selves your Majesties subjects, yett by our present state & being are subject to the authority of the most Illustrious Lords the States Generall) your Majestie shall not only manifest your own piety & justice to the world, but also shall free us, your Majesties humble subjects, from much trouble; & particularly from that perplexity betweene two dangerous extremes whereinto we are cast by being subject in one & the selfe same thing to two severall, distinct, & supreme authorities; whereby it must of necessity follow that some time now or then we must inevitably draw the displeasure of the one or other upon us; it being impossible for us to serve two Masters offending neither.

After this outburst, the ministers more temperately considered the Privy Council's articles one by one, mixing as expediency required the weasel words of Congregational conformity with solid argument in explanation and justification of their acts. With reference to the liturgy they employed, they protested "it never . . . entred into our minds to frame or publish any new Liturgie"; but they confessed they had enlarged from various sources "that [liturgy] all ready extant which by authority & command of the States we are enjoyned to observe." As to their exercise of the power of ordination: "We humbly beseech your Majestie to weigh the nature of ordination, [it] being an essentiall point of the function of our Ministry. . . ." And they went on in good Congregational fashion to argue that the power of ordination was bestowed upon them by Christ and that the King, considering this fact, "will never prohibit us the exercise of anything the power whereof is conferred upon us by Him. . . ." Indeed, as King James had invested them with power to displace ministers, it followed that they had power to ordain them, "Seeing none can displace that have no power to place, nor take away authority where they cannot give it." Further, they dare not grant the power of ordination exclusively "to a forraine Ec-

22 See Appendix II.

3

clesiasticall power" and thus appear to make Holland subject
to "a forraine Authority." Such a practice would endanger
Holland and create a dislike for and mistrust of the Church of
England in Dutch eyes—and they reminded the Privy Council
that "all usurpation of authority over other churches in a
forrain state" was "merely papall" but that even "the Popes
owne law doth not permit a Bishop to ordaine any without the limits of his owne Bishoprick, much lesse in a
forraine state. . . ." Again, if the ministers of the classis
gave up the power of ordination, they would be in a position
inferior to the French in Holland "& so exposed to the prophane
derision & contempt of all men"; they would appear ungrate-
ful to the Dutch who had also invested them with the power;
and they would surrender their primary *raison d'être* in the
Dutch estimation and become "no Churches att all" or be
absorbed completely into the Dutch Reformed Church. Finally,
as the English churches in Holland never have refused ministers ordained in England or in Scotland, they dare not refuse
ministers ordained by the Dutch, "it arguing plainly a professed
separation from them." Concerning the remaining items of
the Privy Council's articles, the ministers denied the introduction of any novelties in rites or ceremonies, "since we have
practised nothing but that which we are able to justifie to be
both commendable, comely, & conforme[-able] to ancient &
present practice . . . "; they protested "there is not a man that
hath beene so much as tainted with any the least surmize either
of Popery or Arminianisme, or any other erroneous sect in
any point of doctrine"; and ironically—considering the charges
current in England against Charles and his ministers—they
"Thank God from our hearts for your Majesties religious care
to have the truth maintained & error avoided" in point of
doctrine.

By such verbal turnings and twistings and by skilfully
playing Dutch authority against English, the ministers of the
classis sought to hide the fact that they conformed neither to
Anglican nor to Dutch Reformed ecclesiastical order. The
Dutch States General, to whom copies of all the correspondence were transmitted in translation, took no action and placed
the communications in their archives without comment.[23] But

23 See above, footnotes 20, 21.

the English Privy Council was not deceived, and the King forbade the classis further to assemble. However, it is unlikely that the order was obeyed, for Carleton, now Viscount Dorchester, was recalled and, temporarily, England had no ambassador to the Dutch Netherlands.[24] Furthermore, upon the petition of John Forbes, the King relented, in part at least, soon afterwards. For in 1629, when Sir Henry Vane was dispatched on a special embassy to Holland, he was instructed to consult the ministers and in case

. . . you find them (as Forbes doth assure they are) more moderate, and temperate, and that they can hold themselves to the first intention of their meetings to see that no Schisme in Doctrine, nor scandall in manners grow amongst them without taking to them selves the liberty of creating Ministers, or framing new Liturgies, or translating the Dutch into English, and that they doe nothing Cross or Contrary to our Church Government here in England, wee like well you should give them all help towards their maintenance and allow their meetings once yearly: . . . [25]

Evidently the ministers convinced Sir Henry of the innocence of their intentions and the Congregational classis successfully weathered this first storm of official disapproval. But it was not for long. English official interest in the classis had scarcely been quieted when a controversy arose to compel Dutch attention and arouse their opposition to the Congregational classis.

This dispute pertained to the choice of a successor to Thomas Potts, associated since 1617 with John Paget in the English church at Amsterdam. Though both Potts and Paget had refused to join the English Congregational classis and affiliated instead with the Dutch Reformed hierarchy, a considerable number of their church members subscribed to Congregational tenets. Accordingly, shortly after Potts died in 1630, Stephen Oswood, "an Inn Keeper dwelling neer the old church at Amsterdam" and a member of Paget's church, wrote a letter on behalf of his fellow Congregationalists in the church to invite Thomas Hooker to the Amsterdam charge with Paget.[26] Hooker, later of Connecticut fame, was then a

24 *Dictionary of National Biography*, article on "Sir Dudley Carleton, Viscount Dorchester."
25 King Charles to Sir Henry Vane, Westminster, Nov. 1629, in *State Papers 16*, vol. 152, fol. 74 (Public Record Office, London). Extracts printed in Appendix VII.
26 *Boswell Papers*, I, fol. 146. Printed in Appendix IX.

popular Congregational lecturer at Chelmsford, Essex, who had just been silenced for nonconformity by one of the English ecclesiastical courts. Doubtless thankful for the opportunity of such ready employment in exile, Hooker indicated his interest in the position and went to visit his friend, Hugh Peter, recently established in the Merchant Adventurers' church at Rotterdam, where he awaited a formal "call" in the Congregational fashion from the elders of the Amsterdam church.

In the meantime, Paget, learning of the business, had become annoyed at the irregularity of the preceedings[27] and, because of Hooker's immediate background and associates, suspicious of his doctrines.[28] Accordingly, Paget insisted that Hooker be examined on various doctrinal questions, but the elders, encouraged by Hugh Peter and others of the Congregational classis, proceeded formally to "call" Hooker to the charge. Thereupon Paget drew up "20 Propositions" for Hooker's consideration and when the elders still refused to be balked in their choice, Paget translated into Latin his "Propositions" and Hooker's replies thereto and placed them before the Dutch classis of Amsterdam.[29] The Dutch ministers debated Hooker's replies and on October 6, 1631, gave it as their opinion that Hooker "could not with edification be allowed hereafter to preach to the English Church in this city."[30] This action settled the issue in the eyes of Paget and the Dutch authorities and Hooker, having another prospect, had already given up hope for the Amsterdam position.[31] But the elders of Paget's church, concurring with Hooker's own Congregational opinion that "a particular congregation hath compleate power, by Christ his institution, to give a compleat call to a Minister without any derived power from a Classis" and, in-

27 According to Paget, ''The Synods of these Reformed Churches, describing the Order to be observed in the Calling of Ministers, do require a choice to be made by the Elders and Deacons; approbation by the Magistrates; allowance of the Classis; and, in the last place, consent of the Congregation . . . '' See Benjamin Hanbury, *Memorials*, I, 539.

28 Hooker's case before the English bishops had made a great noise in England. See *Calendar of State Papers, Dom. Ser., Chas. I, 1628-29*, 554; *ibid., 1629-31*, 87, 92, 567; T. W. Davids, *Annals of Evangelical Nonconformity in the County of Essex* (London, 1863), 154.

29 Paget's ''20 Propositions'' with Hooker's replies appear in *Boswell Papers*, I, fols. 67-72. They are printed in Appendix VIII.

30 Paget's account in Hanbury, *Memorials*, I, 532; but see also *Acta Classis Amstelodamensis*, IV, 9-9b (Amsterdam).

31 *See* the concluding paragraph to his ''Answers'' to Paget's propositions, Appendix VIII.

deed, *"without or against* the Approbation of the Classis,"[32] persisted in their efforts to institute Hooker in their church. At this point, also, John Forbes, as representative of the Congregational classis, undertook to support Hooker's candidacy and demanded of the Dutch classis reasons why they had excepted against Hooker. The Dutch ministers gave him individual answers in writing, but "Mr. Forbes not being satisfied with these Exceptions, writt an Expostulatory letter to the [Dutch] Classis."[33] At this, the Dutch ministers became exasperated and sent Forbes "a sharpe answer reprehending his meddling in things above his place, & plainly blaming the arrogancy of his spirit"; and Jacob Laurentius told him bluntly "that though he complain against the bishops of England, yet [he] himself hath more than an episcopal spirit."[34] Forbes then withdrew in anger, but Hooker's case had already dragged on for months and was not concluded until Paget and the Dutch classis at Amsterdam took the matter before the South Holland Synod which, on September 7, 1632, upheld the previous judgment of the Amsterdam classis.[35] Meanwhile Hooker had become Forbes's assistant at Delft[36] much to the dissatisfaction of the Dutch authorities, who understood by the terms of the Congregational classis's commission from the States General that the English churches were to receive no ministers found unacceptable to the Dutch.

Hooker's replies to John Paget's "20 Propositions" went far to show the Dutch ecclesiastical authorities wherein and to what extent the Congregational ministers differed from themselves and from the Anglicans. For instance, Hooker indicated a willingness to communicate with Brownists and others who had separated from the Church of England; and he would permit members of his church to attend Separatists' sermons without censure. He was not opposed to all use of set forms of prayer, but, unlike the English and Dutch Reformed churches, he was unwilling to baptize infants whose

32 Italics added. See Hooker's reply to the eleventh proposition, Appendix VIII.
33 *Boswell Papers,* I, fol. 146. Appendix IX.
34 *Ibid.,* and *Calendar of State Papers, Dom. Ser., Chas. I, 1633-34,* 30. Published in part in *Proceedings* of the Mass. Hist. Society, XLII, 216.
35 Paget in Hanbury, *Memorials,* I, 532.
36 Hooker remained at Delft until July, 1633, when he departed for New England. In the meantime, he assisted William Ames in composing the latter's *A Fresh Suit Against Ceremonies.* See Cotton Mather, *Magnalia,* I, 308; *Transactions* of the Colonial Society of Mass., XIV, 66.

parents were not members of a reformed church. He believed that it was lawful to employ in church a reader who was not an ordained minister and, to the horror of Paget and his Dutch colleagues, he held that private men might lawfully, in certain circumstances, teach and preach the Gospel. But that which probably most affected the Dutch ministers was Hooker's opinion with regard to the powers of classes and synods over particular congregations. Not only did he maintain that a particular congregation might call a minister "without or against the Approbation of the Classis," but also he concurred completely with Dr. Ames's opinions about the powers of classes in general —which was tantamount to a rejection of all their authority over particular congregations except, as Congregational doctrines allowed, to "counsel and advise." By his skilful examination of Hooker, Paget, who had been aware of these differences for some time, informed Dutch ecclesiastics just what enormities the Congregational men would commit, and from the time of Hooker's case onward Dutch authorities were shaking their heads concernedly over the wisdom of permitting these foreign ministers an independent classis of their own. Forbes's impolitic interference on Hooker's behalf had served only to heighten this feeling. Thus, before the end of 1632 both English and Dutch ecclesiastical officials were aroused over the presumptuous and unorthodox proceedings of the Congregational classis in the Netherlands. Given another dispute to provoke official investigations, the classis might easily find its independent legal status imperilled. Almost before the echoes of Hooker's case had died away that dispute was precipitated—and at John Forbes's church of the Merchant Adventurers at Delft.

CHAPTER III

TROUBLE AT DELFT

Edward Misselden, Deputy at Delft appointed by the Court of the Merchant Adventurers in Hamburg, was a proud and ambitious man. A merchant and writer of economic treatises,[1] he had served the English East India Company as private negotiator with the Dutch with reference to the bitter Amboyna dispute and other East Indian affairs. But he was unsuccessful as a private ambassador and so conducted his affairs as to be suspected of double-dealing both by English and Dutch authorities.[2] Adversity made him petulant, but he could become arrogant in an office of authority; and he was always anxious to please officials in high places. He was a loyal Anglican on occasion, especially if that occasion offered an opportunity for him to recommend himself to the English Privy Council. And so it came about in 1632, after nine years as Deputy at Delft in association with John Forbes, that Misselden, challenged in his authority, chose to report Forbes's nonconformity—and that of the entire membership of the Congregational classis—to the Privy Council in London.

He acted not without provocation. A dispute had arisen in the autumn of 1631 between Forbes and the elders and deacons of his Delft church on the one hand and Misselden and his assistants on the other over membership in the church. According to Misselden, records of the acts of the Court of Deputies of the Company for October, 1631, showed that "at the last Election of Elders & deacons, divers handicraftsmen and others unfree of this fellowship were admitted as members of the Congregation to have their voices with the brethren of the Companie in the said Election."[3] These proceedings

---

1 *Free Trade, or the Means to make Trade Flourish* (1622) and *The Circle of of Commerce, or the Balance of Trade, in Defence of Free Trade, opposed to Malynes* (1623).
2 *Dictionary of National Biography*: "Edward Misselden."
3 *Boswell Papers*, I, fols. 54-55. Printed in Appendix X. It is possible that Forbes was attempting to limit the right to vote in the Company to "the elect," *i. e.*, to Delft Adventurers who were church members in good standing in a manner similar to that enforced upon the Massachusetts Bay electorate in the previous year.

the Deputy felt tended "to the prejudice of the priviledges granted to this fellowship." Thereupon Misselden examined what instructions existed concerning the chaplain's duties and resolved

. . . to confer with Mr. Forbes & the Elders to look back what order & direction they have received from the Companie for the governement of the Church, & to let the Companie have a copie thereof; to the end they may consider of them & in case they finde any Inconvenience by them in these times, they may consider how the same may be redressed.[4]

Forbes was exceedingly anxious that such an investigation and advertisement to the Company should not come to pass; and, at the next Court (November 12, 1631) he agreed with the Deputy that persons not of the Company should have no voice in the management of church affairs and "promised to take care thereof for the future." These assurances appeased Misselden who signified at the next Court (December 26, 1631) that "according to the passage of the last Court concerning church governement, he intended to have let the matter rest."[5] But at this point Forbes, in his anxiety, overplayed his hand. In an effort to make certain that the Deputy interfere no further in church affairs, he and his elders desired a conference with Misselden which only aggravated the situation. Probably they reminded the Deputy that the Company's charter gave neither him nor the Courts ecclesiastical authority to supervise them and they may have paraded their ecclesiastical independence by virtue of the English and Dutch grants to the Congregational classis. In any event, the discussion appears to have become heated, Forbes gave Misselden a lecture on ecclesiastical polity, and the elders accused the Deputy of seeking "to alter the course they are now in & to have the Church governed by the Governor [of the Company] or his Deputy & Assistants." Misselden denied any such intention but asserted "That it had grieved him much that, being in authority, the minister & Elders never advised with him in any thing concerning the church." He went on to indicate, however, that he expected them thereafter "to hold a loving correspondence with him, & therefore he wished the Companie to give all respect & reverence to them in their places." Moreover, the Deputy later propounded the question to the Company, "whether

4 *Ibid.*
5 *Ibid.*

the government of the Church should continue as heretofore
without any change?" And the Court resolved in the affirmative.[6]

Misselden's attitude convinced Forbes that the Deputy was
determined to make the government of the church subservient,
in a measure at least, to that of the Company. Such a thing
was intolerable to the minister and elders and destructive of
the Congregational system. In an effort to ward off the danger,
Forbes and his elders determined to undermine Misselden's
authority as Deputy at Delft and to secure his dismissal. Consequently, early in 1632, they made appeals both to the Dutch
States General and to the Chief Court of the Merchant Adventurers at Hamburg. To the former they reported that
Misselden had performed offices harmful to Dutch trading
interests, that he was seeking to bring in innovations in religion
and to make the Merchant Adventurers' churches subservient
to the authority and laws of England. The States General
made haste (April 16, 1632) to request their ambassadors in
England to employ all their arts to the end that Misselden be
recalled or forced out of the Court at Delft.[7] To the Company's
Court at Hamburg the Delft churchmen had a splendid entrée,
in as much as Samuel Avery, one of the elders in the church,
was son-in-law of the Governor and brother of the Secretary.[8]
Accordingly, as most of the Company at Delft joined with
Forbes against Deputy Misselden, the churchmen made weighty
representations to the Court for his removal. By July, 1632,
Misselden was protesting that though "The Court at Hamburg
re-elected me to this place of government, yet the minister and
Company here continue so violent in their faction and combination that they refuse to come to Courts, and do as those
that said 'Nolumus hunc regnare.' "[9] And at this point the
Deputy, as a matter of self defense, appealed over the heads of
the Court at Hamburg to members of the English Privy Council[10] and, possibly at their suggestion, Misselden drew up for

6 *Boswell Papers*, I, fols. 54-55. Printed in Appendix X.
7 *Archief van de Staten-Generaal*: "Registers van ordinaris resolutien" (1632),
No. 581, fol. 190 (The Hague). See also Raymond P. Stearns (ed.), "Letters
and Documents by or relating to Hugh Peter," in *Essex Institute Historical
Collections* (Salem, Mass.), LXXI, No. 4 (Oct. 1935), 318; LXXII, No. 1
(Jan., 1936), 43-44.
8 *Calendar of State Papers, Dom. Ser., Chas. I, 1633-34*, 364.
9 *Earl Cowper's MSS, 12th Report of the Historical Manuscripts Commission*
(London, 1888), Appendix, Part I, 465-66.
10 *Earl Cowper's MSS* in *ibid.*, Appendix, Part I, 465-66, 467-68.

Sir Francis Windebank, Privy Council secretary, a complete
statement of "The Abuses" of the "English Churches in the
Lowe Countries" together with "The Remedies" for them.
On October 29, 1632 (o.s.), he presented these notes in person
before the Privy Council in London.[11]

    Deputy Misselden's account of "The Abuses" transcended
the petty controversy at Delft and struck at all the Congregational churches in Holland and their classis. He informed the
Privy Council

> That there are about 25 or 30 English Churches in the Lowe Coun-
> tries which, for the most part, are Seminaries of disorderly preachers.
> And albeit that some men may think that the Land's well quit of them,
> for that they are beyond the seas, yet there they do more harme than
> they could do here,
>
> In or by { Corrupting our Nation;
>   { Writing scandalous books;
>   { holding Continuall Correspondence with
>   the Refractories of England.

That the Marchants-Adventurers preachers in the Low Countries are the
Chief of those Refractories there. That some of them opposed King
James in Scotland & for which they were banished thence, yet continue
the same opinions in the Low Countries, getting some kind of protection
of the States. They will observe no forms of prayer nor admit any
Liturgy or divine service which is that *cultus Dei* which ought to be in
every Christian Church; they will observe no solemnities, as Xmas day,
the passion day, &c; nor will they administer the Sacraments in any
forme but their owne. They take upon them to plant Churches & ordaine
ministers; & have very much Laboured with His Majesty here & the
States there to have an English Synod, on faire pretences but false grounds
& to serve their owne turnes.

Misselden went on to describe the state of affairs at Delft,
stating that "the Company here [at London] are forced to
send over Commissioners with me to Examine these insolencies
& to Confirme me in my place"; and he warned the Privy
Council that by these occurrences it "may be guessed, as by a
true Scantling, what these of their mind would do against His
Majesties Government here if they durst."

    The Deputy's suggested "Remedies" for these conditions
were even more far-reaching than his statement of "The
Abuses." He proposed that the Dutch authorities be induced
to admit no ministers to the English churches in Holland who

11 *State Papers 16*, Vol. 224, fol. 57 (Public Record Office, London). Printed in
   Appendix XI; briefed in *Cal. of State Papers, Dom. Ser., Chas. I, 1631-33*, 432.

do not conform either to the Church of England or to the Dutch Reformed Church; that these ministers be permitted no independent classis, "by any meanes"; that if the ministers of the Merchant Adventurers' churches would submit "to His Majesties Ecclesiastical Government & to the Companies Government in the affairs of our owne Church, & give due respect to me their Deputy-Governor," they might be "continued in their places"; if they refused, then the Merchant Adventurers should be enjoined by the Privy Council "to send over other reverend, learned, & Conformable Divines in their roomes"; that the new ambassador to the Dutch Netherlands, Sir William Boswell, be instructed to give careful attention to these things, "to Countenance me, the Deputy, in this service," to assist the Company's commissioners about to be sent over with Misselden, and to employ the authority of the English Privy Council if "this faction at Delft cannot be reformed by the authority of the Company." Lastly—and most revolutionary of all—Misselden insisted that the government of the Merchant Adventurers be placed exclusively in the Company's Court at London rather than in the Court at Hamburg, that "the Governor & Deputies be henceforth chosen at London" for the foreign courts in order that "the Government, which is a gemme of the Kings Crown, may be maintained in its owne honor, And then even Strangers . . . will know the Soveraigne at home by the Subject abroad, . . . "

Misselden's memorial and testimony to the Privy Council were sufficient to arouse the English authorities to action. Following the Deputy's recommendations almost to the letter, they permitted the Company's commissioners to try to settle the business, withholding further official action until the outcome of the Company's efforts were known. Two days after Misselden's report, the Privy Council sent a "letter for helping the Commissioners in Mr. Misselden's business & countenancing him in his government."[12] The Lords of the Council,

well knowing of what dangerous consequence this may prove (if it should be suffered) not only in relation to trade but also to his Majesties service and affaires in those parts, doe hereby in his Majesties name especially will and require you to do anything possible by all your best endeavours

12 *Boswell Papers*, I, fols. 58-59. The letter, dated Oct. 31, 1632, was signed by Manchester, Cottington, Windebank, Weston, Edmonds, Sir William Boswell, and Coventry.

unto the said deputy in countenancing and supporting him in the said Government.

Armed with this authority, Misselden and the Company's London commissioners, consisting of "Mr. Law, their deputy; Mr. Stymer, their Secretary; & Mr. Edwards, Lately their Treasurer," went to Delft to discipline John Forbes, his elders, and the merchants who supported them.

The commissioners were embarrassed in their efforts from the first by the temporary absence of Forbes. For the Minister, "having put the Company into this distraction" (as Misselden wrote[13]), had left in July, 1632, on a visit to the army of Gustavus Adolphus, King of Sweden, then in the Germanies.[14] The commissioners could do little with the elders and members of the congregation who simply bided their time until the Company's representatives departed. Moreover, the commissioners were misled by such Congregational alacrity as that displayed by seventeen members of the Delft church who declared to Sir William Boswell, November 27, 1632, that they were ready to take the oaths of supremacy and allegiance whenever required and to conform to all the laws of England when they came to live therein, although in the past they had conformed to the government established in the churches of the United Provinces "by the joint authority of our State as well as of this State."[15] On December 4 the commissioners held a Court at which, according to Misselden, they compelled the Delft congregation "to a conditional conformity" which, the Deputy sourly added, "is to no purpose if it be left there," for the people only wait until the commissioners depart to return

---

13 Misselden to Sir John Coke, Delft, July 26, 1632, in *The Manuscripts of the Earl Cowper, K. G.*, in *Historical Manuscripts Commission, Twelfth Report, Appendix, Part I* (London, 1888), 465-66.

14 With Scottish troops brought to the Continent for Gustavus's use by Marquis Hamilton were kinsmen whom Forbes visited. Also, before he returned to Delft, Forbes was employed by the Swedish Chancellor, Oxenstierna, on some financial errands. See Gilbert Burnet, *The Memoires of the . . . Dukes of Hamilton* (London, 1677), 11-16; John Rushworth, *Historical Collections* (7 vols., London, 1659-1701), II, 53-63, 166-75; James Ferguson (ed.), *Papers Illustrating the History of the Scots Brigade in the Service of the United Netherlands, 1572-1782* (Publications of the Scottish History Society, XXXII, 2 vols., Edinburgh, 1899), I, 310-12; *The Swedish Intelligencer* (London, 1632-33), pt. ii, 145; *Rikskansleren Axel Oxenstiernas Skrifter och Brefvexling . . . Bref 1632* (Stockholm, 1926), VII, 652-54. Nos. 620-21. I am much indebted to Professor Franklin D. Scott of Northwestern University for aid in translating such linguistic hybrids as these letters to Conrad von Falkenberch, svensh Kommissarie i Amsterdam.

15 *Cal. of State Papers, Dom. Ser., Chas. I, 1631-33*, 445.

to their former ways.[16]   Soon afterwards the commissioners
left, taking back to Archbishop Laud in England "four propositions subscribed at Delft" in typical Congregational am-
biguity, to the effect, first, that God's Word is truly preached
and the sacraments rightly administered in the church at Delft;
second, that the discipline used there is according to the Word
of God; third, that they submit to be ruled by their pastor and
elders; and fourth, that whosoever does not submit shall be
held as a heathen and publican.[17]   As Misselden and Laud well
knew—though possibly the Company's representatives did not,
being inexperienced in the peculiarities of Congregational nonconformity—the commissioners had effected nothing of
permanent consequence in the way of bringing the Delft church
to obedience and conformity.

In mid-January, 1633, John Forbes returned to Holland
out of Germany.   His family, together with Thomas Hooker
and Hugh Peter, met him in Amsterdam where they remained
about a week before Forbes went back to Delft.[18]   Misselden
wrote to Boswell that he had learned

. . . by a letter I have seene, written by a bosome friend of his [Forbes]
of discourse had with him at Amsterdam, that he returns the same man
he went out from hence in point of Church differences here.   So if
neither his age, nor journey, nor time, have taken off his dog there's the
more work for you. . . .   And therefore the sooner you set upon it, it
will the better, when there is so much to be done . . . the time, & thing
is pressing . . . there's no hope of Reconciliation.   Such he pretends is
their liberty given them by Christ.[19]

Exactly a week later, after Forbes had returned to Delft, Misselden wrote excitedly to Boswell that he and the minister had
conferred and "the business is in a good way of pacification
between Mr. Forbes & me."[20]   But the Deputy's rejoicing was
premature.   Evidently Forbes had merely been feeling his way
cautiously for, less than a week later, the minister was in
London playing at the Deputy's game—appealing directly to
the English Privy Council.

The chief fruits of Forbes's visit to London are to be
found in a memorial he presented to the Privy Council on

16 *Boswell Papers*, I, fol. 61.
17 *Cal. of State Papers, Dom. Ser., Chas. I, 1633-34*, 317-18.
18 Misselden to Boswell, Delft, Jan. 7/17, 1632/33, *Boswell Papers*, I, fol. 74.
19 Same to Same, Delft, Jan. 10/20, 1632/33, in *ibid.*, I, fol. 76.
20 Same to Same, Delft, Jan. 20/27, 1632/33, in *ibid.*, I, fol. 78.

February 10, 1632/33, entitled "The true nature, state, and ground of the trouble raised by Mr. Deputie Misselden in the Church of the Companie of Marchand Adventurers in Delft."[21] According to Forbes, Misselden, "after divers private attempts," openly opposed "the forme and order of ecclesiasticall government established and practised in this church by mutuall consent of bothe States" and tried "utterly to abolish it as unlawfull and contrarie to the world." That government which the Deputy labors to establish in the Delft church has "no precedent in any church whatsoever" inasmuch as "he claimeth to himself, and that ex officio, as deputie, the whole and sole power of ecclesiastical government in this Church . . ." As "governor," the Deputy claims not only civil authority over the Company but ecclesiastical power over the church and pastor thereof as well, "being, as he alleadgeth, an Elder, or ecclesiastical governour ex officio." Misselden went on to claim that "an elder and a bishop were all one, without any difference, whereupon [said Forbes] this conclusion must follow, that the deputie must be ex officio the bishop of this Church as well as deputie of the Companie. . . . the bishops of England may here see whether it be for them or himself that he stryveth." The Deputy argued from precedents drawn from the "tyme of popery," before the Company had a church, when the Deputies had only domestic chaplains who were subject to their orders, "putting no difference betwixt a private chaplain in a familie and a publick minister of a Congregation." Further, Misselden attacked as "absolutely unlawfull and contrarie to the word of God" the ecclesiastical government of a church which had been legally sanctioned by both the English and Dutch states; and "to make this ground to hold, he layeth heavie reproaches and odious scandals upon it and Mr. Forbes and the Elders," saying that they endeavor "to maintain a presbyteriall government and discipline above the Kings government," that they "goe against our mother church in maintaining and abetting a schismaticall kynd of government"—all of which, said Forbes, showed either "miserable ignorance of the nature of ecclesiasticall and civill government, or malicious prophannes, or prophane malice." Again, the Deputy held that the Company's church "is more eminent, and of greater ex-

21 *Boswell Papers*, I, fols. 89-90. Printed in Appendix XII.

cellencie, than any other Church, and therefore is to be governed in another manner. . . ." By this "all men may see that the deputie stryveth not for any discipline established in any other Church, but for a strange one, in his judgment more excellent . . . and (as shall appear) it is this, that this Church be governed by him and no other." Finally, said Forbes,

I would demand of Mr. deputie, why amongst his other reproachfull calumnies against Mr. Forbes, he accuseth him that he opposeth the government of bishops as not of divine institution; for either this must be the deputies own opinion, or then he must esteem the government that is juro divino to be more base in ecclesiasticall affairs than that which is jure humano; for I doe not think that he will say that he is jure divino ecclesiasticall governour of this church. Let both his Majestie and bishops see what this man ayms at, which in all reason can be nothing else but to take to himself the same supremacie in the Company which is his Majesties Royal prerogative in his dominions and so, in effect, to raigne as King in this Company.
Out of these things men may perceive wherein standeth the excellencie of this church above others in his judgment: 1. In that this church is not to be governed by any minister of Christ designed and ordained by Him in His Word for ruling of his sanctuarie; but by the deputie or governour of the Companie, and so not by an man having his authoritie and calling from Heaven or from Christ, but by a man who hath his authoritie and calling from men. . . . 2. In that this church is not to be governed by any lawes of Christ or His Word, or any decrees of Councils or ecclesiasticall canons of any church whatsoever, popish or reformed, no not of England nor yet of the lawes of the King or State; but only by the private orders of the Companie made by them for ordering themselves in the priviledges of their marchant trade.

Forbes's memorial to the English Privy Council appears to have been written by a man who knew he supported a losing cause. Given before such an unsympathetic audience as the Lords of His Majesty's Council who had not only heard Misselden's weighty charges against the church at Delft and all the English Congregational ministers in Holland but had had occasion to check the veracity of many of them, Forbes's insinuating references to the legality of his ecclesiastical polity as established by mutual consent of both states made the Lords only more anxious to terminate King James's grant to the classis; his attacks upon Misselden's arguments and motives redounded upon himself in the eyes of a Council already pledged to support the Deputy in his place, seemed rather irrelevant to the larger issues laid at the door of the Congregational ministers by Misselden; and if his logic appeared somewhat difficult to follow and a bit tenuous at times, the Lords must have winked knowingly at one another, for they were thoroughly experienced in this type of nonconformist argument "from the Word." And so the memorial and Forbes's appearance before the Council rather confirmed than lessened the Lords' determination not only to establish order—loyal, Anglican order— among the merchants at Delft but also to stamp out the nonconforming practices of the Congregationalists and their classis in the Dutch Netherlands. Soon after Forbes departed, the Privy Council received further evidence of Misselden's orthodox loyalty. The Deputy cited his commissions from the Company "to use the authority of my place in repressing schisme, faction, & disordre in the Church . . . whereby ex officio I am bound not only to reprove but also to reforme what is amisse." But if he had none of these warrants, out of honor to the King and the Church of England he would feel bound in conscience to protest against such a church as that of the Company at Delft. If it were you, he queried, as private men,

with what Conscience could you subscribe to such a Church government . . . as is *neither conformable to the Church of England, nor the Reformed Churches of these Countries, nor to the Church of this city* . . . ? *That hath neither Liturgie, Catechisme, Confession, set formes of prayer, celebration of the Sacraments in any sett forme, exercise of the Lord's Prayer, solemne thankesgivings for the birth & death of Christ &c?* The wants of all which not only tend to the corrupting of our young Merchants which are sent out hither for good education, but to cause strangers that looke upon us to think that the Church of England is as ill governed at home.[22]

However, despite all the Deputy's loyalty and willingness, the fiasco of the Company's commissioners to Delft demonstrated to the Privy Council that more than the authority and prestige of the Merchant Adventurers was necessary to eradicate the intrenched nonconformity of the English ministers to the Company and to the English soldiers in Holland. His Majesty's government must take a hand directly, and no more effective instrument could have been employed than the Resident Ambassador lately appointed to the Low Countries.

22 *Boswell Papers*, I, fol. 124. Printed in Appendix XIII.

CHAPTER IV

THE AMBASSADOR'S FOURFOLD TASK

I

William Boswell arrived at The Hague as successor to Sir Dudley Carleton in August, 1632, about the time the dispute between Edward Misselden and the Delft congregation was reaching its most heated phase. Although East Anglian, and Cambridge educated, Boswell was no Puritan. A zealous supporter of the royal prerogative and of the Established Church, he had had experience both in diplomacy and in the ways of Puritan nonconformity.[1] He had attended the Earl of Carlisle on a diplomatic expedition to Lorraine and Piedmont; he had been associated with Carleton in his ambassadorial duties in Holland; and, both as secretary to the Bishop of Lincoln and as servant to the Archbishop of Canterbury, he had been unusually efficient in ferreting out Puritans.[2] Unlike the commissioners of the Merchant Adventurers' Court at London sent with Misselden in the autumn of 1632 to attempt to straighten the tangled affairs of the Delft church, Boswell was acquainted with the wiles and ambiguous protestations of Congregational nonconformists. He lent all his support to the commissioners' dismal efforts and was repeatedly urged by Deputy Misselden to take a direct hand in the proceedings even before the commissioners returned to London.[3] When news arrived that John Forbes had returned from the Germanies in January, 1633, Misselden implored Boswell "to prepare for his coming";[4] and after Forbes's arrival, the Deputy, anticipating that his work would now proceed "more efficaciously in England than ever I have yet done," notified the Ambassador that, "I solemnly expect two things of you especially: The

---

1 See the sketch of Boswell in Appendix A.
2 John Hacket, *Scrinia Reserata* (London, 1693), Part I, 86.
3 See letters of Misselden to Boswell, Delft, Dec. 4, 1632; Dec. 8, 1632; Dec.?, 1632; Jan. 7/17, 1632/33; and Jan. 26, 1632/33, in *Boswell Papers*, I, fols. 61, 63, 73, 74, and 80 respectively.
4 Misselden to Boswell, Jan. 7/17, 1632/33. *Boswell Papers*, I, fol. 74.

4

one, that you will not suffer Mr. Forbes or any of his party to draw out the time too much at length, which haply of their skill may exceedingly prejudice me & the cause too; the other, that you will not receive protestations without Examination & hearing what I can say against the same."[5]   Indeed, the Deputy's meticulous demands sometimes bordered upon insubordination and, though Boswell undertook the task of bringing the English ministers in Holland to conformity as the Privy Council had directed, he was forced to reprimand Misselden for his importunities.[6]

Boswell faced a delicate and difficult task. As he wrote in his first report to the Privy Council, "our English Ministers & Church affayres in these parts" are such that "at my first entry & view I spied to be a spider of divers threads, uneven, very much entangled, & requiring tyme to cleene them handsomely for his Majesty's honor & service without raysing of dust in my owne or others Eyes."[7]   The Ambassador was responsible to the English Privy Council which, in ecclesiastical affairs, was governed largely by William Laud; and the Bishop was exceedingly anxious to end the nonconformity among the English merchants and soldiers in the Netherlands.   Yet he had to give careful attention to the Dutch authorities who were more than half inclined to believe the Congregational ministers' repeated protestations that the English attempts to enforce conformity meant not only unwarranted foreign interference in Dutch internal affairs but also the extension to Holland of unreformed, popish ecclesiastical ways.   Moreover, the Ambassador had need of caution in view of the legal security from both Dutch and English interference which the Congregational classis had by treaty, royal grant, Dutch commission, the nature of the organization of the Merchant Adventurers, and the peculiar type of nonconformity which obligingly permitted Congregationalists to take the oath of supremacy and to admit that the Church of England was a true church. Further, public sentiment among the soldiers and the Merchant Adventurers in Holland widely supported the nonconforming preachers and their classis, as was well demonstrated in the summer of 1633

5 Same to same, Jan. 26, 1632/33. *Boswell Papers*, I, fol. 80.
6 Same to same, March 7, 1632/33. *Boswell Papers*, I, fols. 99-100; see also *ibid.*, I, fols. 80, 96.
7 Dispatch to Secretary Coke, March 8/18, 1632/33. In *Boswell Papers*, I, fols. 116-19. Printed in Appendix XIV.

when, despite all the pressure from England, the Court at Hamburg removed Edward Misselden from his position as Deputy at Delft and installed John Forbes's elder, Samuel Avery, in his stead.[8] All these circumstances convinced Boswell of the necessity for carefully planned, well founded proceedings. Accordingly, while Misselden chafed for action and eventually lost his place at Delft, the Ambassador set out systematically to collect information about the affairs of the English churches in Holland: to gather proofs of their nonconformity, of their seditious acts and speeches, of their printing and disseminating in England as well as in the Netherlands of "scandalous" books, of their illegal ordination of ministers, and of their failure to live up to the conditions of ecclesiastical orderliness imposed upon them by the Dutch commission for the Congregational classis. Meanwhile, Laud kept a sharp lookout for their letters and pamphlets in England.

In his search for facts, Boswell was greatly assisted from the outset by Deputy Misselden who had spent a decade in close association with the Merchant Adventurers in the Netherlands. But in addition to the Delft Deputy, a number of disgruntled ministers and laymen supplied the Ambassador with valuable data. Strangely enough, John Paget, who had been exiled for nonconformity in the reign of James I, was so incensed over the case of Thomas Hooker and related matters that he joined forces with the English Ambassador to inform against the Congregational classis and its members. And Alexander Brown, a member of Hugh Peter's Rotterdam congregation, Charles Kettleby, a soldier, and Stephen Goffe, chaplain to Lord Vere and student at the University of Leiden, were useful men in Boswell's service.

Of all these informers, Stephen Goffe, who had first been brought to Boswell's attention by Edward Misselden,[9] was the most effectively active. Though son of a Puritan minister and brother of William Goffe, later the Puritan regicide,[10] Goffe

8 *Calendar of State Papers, Dom. Ser., Chas. I, 1633-34*, 152-53; *Add. MSS 17677 O*, fols. 101-103. Letter from Govert Brasser to the States General, London, Aug. 17, 1633.

9 See Misselden to Boswell, Dec. 4, 1632, and Dec.?, 1632, in *Boswell Papers*, I, fols. 61, 73.

10 Stephen Goffe (1605-1681) was son of Stephen, Sr., a Puritan minister in Sussex. Stephen, Jr., aspired to become a great theological scholar. He graduated B.A. at Merton College, Oxford, in 1624, and M.A. at St. Alban's Hall, Oxford, in 1627. About 1632 he became chaplain to Lord Vere's regiment

was a loyal Anglican who had his own reasons for disliking the Congregational classis in Holland. In the summer of 1632, Lord Vere, acting upon instructions from England, gave orders to his chaplain, Goffe, to read "the prayers of the Church of England after the forme there used."[11] Goffe responded gladly, but he was opposed by Colonel Hollis and some of the army chaplains, notably by Samuel Batchelor, member and secretary of the Congregational classis and chaplain to Colonel Morgan's regiment. These men informed the Dutch States of the proceedings, "and that by way of intimation of fault as if some new and Superstitious thing had been introduced." The Dutch authorities ordered Goffe to translate the prayers into Dutch and to present them for inspection, cut off his salary, and Goffe found it very difficult to convince them that he was not "an Innovator and dangerous troubler of the Church." Meanwhile, the Congregational classis showered admonitions both upon Goffe and the Dutch authorities, and it was several months before the chaplain freed himself of the troublesome tangle initiated by his innocent and obedient use of the Book of Common Prayer. Consequently, Goffe was delighted to serve as informer against his tormentors.[12]

in the Low Countries and carried on studies in theology at the University of Leiden (matriculated Feb. 20, 1633) with Ludovick de Dieu. About 1638 Goffe returned to England, later became chaplain to Charles I, and procured a D.D. at the King's instance. During the English Civil Wars, Goffe did yeoman services in the Low Countries for the King, collecting monies and patching up diplomatic fences. He served as chaplain to exiled Queen Henrietta Maria, tried to marry the wild Prince Charles (later Charles II) to the daughter of the Prince of Orange, was tutor to young James Croft, later Duke of Monmouth. After the establishment of the Commonwealth in England, Goffe gave up in despair, turned Roman Catholic, entered the Congregation of French Oratory in the seminary of Notre Dame des Vertus near Paris (Jan., 1650), and remained there until his death on Christmas day, 1681. He was respected as a scholar, wrote *Nine Latin Epistles* addressed to Vossius, the Dutch theologian. For references, see Anthony Wood, *Athenae Oxoniensis* in *Fasti Oxoniensis* (1721 edition), 227, 236, 271; *Dictionary of National Biography; Album Studiosorum Academiae Lugduno Batavae MDLXXV-MDCCCLXXV* (The Hague, 1875), column 250; "Journal of Occurrences," in *Add. MSS 25, 465* (B.M., London), fol. 48; Letter of Ludovick de Dieu to Goffe, Leiden, March 28, 1633, in *Papenbroek MSS* (Leiden University Library), 2 (D); and fifteen letters by Goffe to Constantine Huygens, Monsieur Seigneur de Zulicum, Councillor and Secretary to the Prince of Orange, in *Huygens MSS, 37, G,* (Leiden University Library).

11 Stephen Goffe to Henry Earl of Dover, Feb. 7, 1633, in *State Papers 16*, vol. 232, fol. 23 (Public Record Office, London); briefed in *Cal. of State Papers, Dom. Ser., Chas. I, 1631-33*, 530. See also Goffe to Boswell, March 10, 1633, in *Boswell Papers*, I, fol. 107. Printed in Appendix XV. An interesting memorandum in the *Boswell Papers* (I, fol. 172) adds corroborative evidence.

12 *Calendar of State Papers, Dom. Ser., Chas. I, 1631-33*, 530, 554; *Boswell Papers*, I, fol. 73.

II

Four closely interrelated tasks, as Boswell's report to the Privy Council shows,[13] confronted the Ambassador and his corps of assistants. The first was to reduce the merchants at Delft to order and conformity; the second was to enforce conformity upon the English soldiers in the Dutch service; the third— which was the key to the others—was to find positive proofs of the disloyalty and nonconformity of the Congregational classis as a basis for the withdrawal of the liberty granted the ministers for its organization in 1621; and the fourth was to induce the States General to rescind their commission to the classis—an accomplishment contingent upon persuading Dutch civil and ecclesiastical authorities both that the English intended no dangerous and unwarranted interference in Dutch ecclesiastical affairs and that the Congregational classis was a positive menace both to Dutch ecclesiastical order and to English merchants and soldiers in the Netherlands.

To effect the first of these was a troublesome and thankless chore, especially as John Forbes was a skilful opponent supported by a loyal congregation whose ire was up because of Deputy Misselden's meddlesome arrogance. Boswell soon discovered, after a series of talks with Forbes, that there was no hope of reconciling the differences between the church and Deputy Misselden. Accordingly, the Ambassador "playnely" told Forbes "that his Majestie had taken a resolution (as he had reason) in his own Peculiars . . . to have Divine Service performed according to the Lawes of his owne Church & Kingdome: And that I should be very glad to see him, a mann of gravity & Creditt amongst our English Ministers in these Countries, beginn an Example of so good a worke."[14] Forbes replied "That he knewe too well his duty to God & the King to oppose his Majestye or speake agaynst his purpose herein" but "his age did call uppon him to retire & rest, which he proposed to doe & meant very speedily to acquaynt the Company therewith that they might provide another in his place." To be sure, Forbes was approaching the age of sixty-five years, but he was not too old temporarily to block the Ambassador's

13 See Appendix XIV.
14 See Appendix XIV.

attempts to remove him by throwing every possible obstacle in his way.   When Boswell requested a conference, Forbes procrastinated;[15] when Boswell demanded to see the Delft church's Registry Book, the pastor and elders demurred on the ground that it might give rise to scandals and that, by the canons of their discipline, such information, like confession, was strictly private.[16]   Accordingly, the Ambassador, in order to inform the Privy Council of the constitution of the Delft church, was forced to fall back upon the evidence of Misselden and his other informers.[17]   Moreover, when Forbes was hard pressed, he invariably fell back upon the Congregational classis for support and Thomas Hooker, his assistant, gave him "diligent advice" to stand firm in his own way at Delft or to "go for New England," as Hooker himself did before the summer of 1633 had passed.[18]

Forbes and the congregation at Delft did stand firm throughout most of 1633 and it was Misselden, as has been stated above, who was forced to retire from the Company at Delft (July, 1633).   And this was in spite of King Charles's specific order to the Company of Merchant Adventurers (May 29, 1633) to the effect that, "Whereas the King's intention never was that any company residing in foreign parts should exempt themselves from the government of this Church and State.   The King therefore wills the Company not to entertain any Minister departed from this Country or censured here for nonconformity, but only such as are conformable."[19]   Again, October 1, 1633, by an order of the King in Council, the Merchant Adventurers were enjoined not to receive any ministers into their churches in foreign parts without His Majesty's approbation of their persons.[20]   Still, Forbes stayed on at Delft

15 See, for example, Misselden's letter to Boswell, Delft, Feb. 19/29, 1632/33, in *Boswell Papers*, I, fol. 96.
16 Letter of Jan Quarles to Boswell, March 2/12, 1632/33, in *Boswell Papers*, I, fols. 108-109. When they got the Register Book later they found in it nothing about the church's discipline and were inclined to agree with Forbes and the elders, in as much as the book contained "only certaine Ecclesiasticall censures used by the Church against cousenage, swearing, Drunkness, raylings, fornications, etc." See same to same, Delft, March 2, 1632/33, in *ibid.*, I, fols. 103-104.
17 Misselden to Boswell, Delft, March 7, 1632/33, in *Boswell Papers*, I, fols. 99-100; *Cal. of State Papers, Dom. Ser., Chas. I, 1631-33*, 575.
18 Misselden to Boswell, Delft, March 20/30, 1632-33, in *Boswell Papers*, I, fol. 121.
19 *Cal. of State Papers, Dom. Ser., Chas. I, 1633-34*, 74-75.
20 *Ibid.*, 225.

and Stephen Goffe reported in November that Forbes boasted of victory over Boswell "and though another be to come in his place (one Dr. Sibbald they say) yet he is to be but as it were the Curate & that Mr. Forbes shall still be entertained as the preacher, which (I use the words of one of the merchants) is the choice work . . . And thus Mr. Forbes will find as good Entertainment as before, . . ."[21]   However, Archbishop Laud was becoming exasperated.   On December 11, 1633, he assured Boswell that "Mr. Forbes shall never come thither againe, unlesse he will conforme himself in all things, which I knowe he will not doe, at least in that place."[22]   Forbes was still at Delft late in December, 1633,[23] but in January following he was called to London to appear before Archbishop Laud.   Evidently Laud handled him with more tact than he usually displayed toward nonconformists, for Forbes departed "with much content of the Bishop," and promised to take no further part in the ministry of the Delft church.[24]

Forbes's successor in the Delft church, as planned by the King, Laud, Misselden, and others, was none other than Stephen Goffe himself.   But Goffe was vehemently opposed to the appointment because, as he wrote, of "the intollerable burthen of the place; they have been used to heare three Extemporary sweating sermons every weeke, and so unlesse I bring them at least two sermons I shall never be reckoned a preacher amongst them.   And I must confesse I cannot see how it is possible for me to performe that, unlesse I should descend to that unconscionable fashion of theirs in talking whatever offers itselfe."[25]   Goffe also appealed to Boswell, "Oh, Sir, for God sake free me from this feare & let me know what misery is falling upon me, & which of my faults hath brought me this

21 Goffe to ?, The Hague, Nov. 7/17, 1633, in *State Papers 16*, vol. 250, fol. 28 (P. R. O., London); see also Alexander Browne to Boswell, Rotterdam, Nov. 1, 1633, in *Boswell Papers*, I, fol. 153.   Largely printed in Burrage, *Early English Dissenters*, II, 272-73, and in *Proceedings* of the Mass. Hist. Society, XLII, 222-23.
22 Laud to Boswell, Lambeth, Dec. 11, 1633 (o.s.) in *Papenbroek MSS 2* (L) (University of Leiden Library, Holland).   Printed in Appendix XVI.
23 Goffe to William Brough, The Hague, Dec. 16/26, 1633, in *State Papers 16*, vol. 252, fol. 55 (P.R.O., London).
24 *Cal. of State Papers, Dom. Ser., Chas. I, 1633-34*, 406, 447.
25 Goffe to Gilbert Sheldon, Leiden, Feb. 3/13, 1633/34, in *State Papers 16*, vol. 260, fol. 13 (P. R. O. London); briefed in *Cal. of State Papers, Dom. Ser., Chas. I, 1633-34*, 449-50.

plague."[26]   Finally, he was able to turn it down without official offense, and in June, 1634, George Beaumont was installed as minister to Forbes's former charge.[27]   Forbes preached secretly now and then until late in 1634 when he died.   In the next year, too, the chief court of the Merchant Adventurers in the Low Countries was moved from Delft to Rotterdam.   The transfer was made partly as a result of the Rotterdam merchants' desire for a monopoly of the cloth trade at their mart and partly as a result of the Privy Council's desire to restrict the merchants further in their church affairs.   Negotiations for the change began in 1634 and they were concluded in February, 1635, with the signing of a concordat between the Company and the city of Rotterdam.   By this concordat, the city officials agreed to set aside St. Peter's Church for the use of the English company and specified that religious exercises performed therein were to be "according to the discipline and order of the Church of England."[28]   In the same year, upon the King's recommendation, Samuel Avery was discharged as Deputy of the Merchant Adventurers.   The King pressed the reappointment of Misselden, but the merchants protested, and finally a compromise candidate, Richard Bladwell, was selected for the place.[29]   With Avery's discharge, the last vestige of the influence of John Forbes's party passed from power.   The first of Ambassador Boswell's tasks was completed.

III.

In undertaking his second, the Ambassador was materially assisted by the information collected by Stephen Goffe who, as the chaplain of Lord Vere's regiment, had been balked in the use of the English Book of Common Prayer.   Samuel Batchelor, chaplain to Colonel Morgan's regiment, had been the chief instrument in opposing Goffe's action, had enlisted the support of the Congregational classis, had aroused the Dutch authorities to discipline Goffe, and, consequently, was the chief object of

26 Goffe to Boswell, Feb. 5/15, 1633/34, in *Boswell Papers*, I, fol. 180.
27 *Cal. of State Papers, Dom. Ser., Chas. I, 1634-35*, 87.
28 *Cal. of State Papers, Dom. Ser., Chas. I, 1635-36*, 34-36; Appendix XIV; *Earl Cowper MSS*, in *12th Report of the Hist. MSS Comm.*, II, Appendix II, 69; C. T. Lintum, *De Merchant Adventurers in de Nederlanden* (The Hague, 1905), 237-63.
29 *Cal. of State Papers, Dom. Ser., Chas. I, 1635*, 151; *ibid., 1635-36*, 36-37, 302; *Boswell Papers*, I, fol. 208.

Goffe's, Boswell's, and the Privy Council's attention.[30]   But Batchelor had support from his colonel and others in the army, notably Colonels Herbert and Hollis.   Goffe, with Boswell's diplomatic connivance, merely waited until the Dutch authorities' storm of disapproval subsided to resume his use of the Prayer Book.   Lord Vere, having explicit orders from the Privy Council, countenanced his chaplain's proceedings and was congratulated by the Privy Council for maintaining true English church forms among the soldiers in Holland.[31]   At the same time, the Privy Council ordered Colonel Morgan and Colonel Herbert to conform and to send their chaplains to England for interrogation.[32]   The colonels obeyed—on the surface at least—and Morgan discharged Batchelor from his chaplaincy.   But Batchelor did not go to England.   Maintaining that Dutch authorities refused to allow the Prayer Book's use, he retired to his home at Gorinchem and engaged the Congregational classis to induce the Dutch States to put a stop to the extension of the Established Church service to the English soldiers.[33]

Meanwhile, Boswell and his agents sought a man as Batchelor's successor.   Goffe settled upon one Mr. Grim, minister to a small English church at Wesel.   Grim was a German who had studied at Oxford, had recently taken his degree at Leiden, where he had written a thesis in support of the English liturgy.   Goffe wrote that Grim

30 *See* Appendix XIV.
31 John Coke to Lord Vere, Whitehall Feb. 15, 1632/33, in *Boswell Papers*, I, fol. 91.
32 *Ibid.;* also Coke to Morgan, Feb. 14, 1632/33, in *ibid.*, I, fol. 84.   Coke informed Morgan that His Majesty had learned that ''a Minister of your regiment, Mr. Bachelor, not only refuses himselfe to reade prayers according to the forme of the book of Common Prayers authorized by law; but to give interruption to others that therein conforme themselves.   In this his Majestie findeth no small dishonor . . . to our Church and State. . . . His Majestie requireth . . . speedily to send over into England the said Mr. Bachelor, heere to give account of his Proceedings and to be informed better. And from your self his Majestie doth expect that you shall not henceforth countenance any such refractorie person, but rather entertaine such as are obedient to law and discipline of our Church there. . . .'' *See* also Coke to Col. Hollis in *Cal. of State Papers, Dom. Ser., Chas. I, 1631-33*, 554.
33 John Coke to Col. Morgan, London, April 2, 1633, in *Boswell Papers*, I, fol. 126; Coke wrote that His Majesty assumed that the Dutch states will not ''interpose at all for protection of any of his Subjects against his regal power over them nor doe any thinge in prejudice of our Church government amongst his Majesties Subjects there, considering the liberties their Subjects enjoy here, which they would not willinglie have restrained.   Mr. Boswell hath directions to treat with them as he findeth Cause, & particularly to press them to let Batchelor come over, . . . ''; see also John Simson to Boswell, Leiden, April 9, 1633, in *ibid.*, I, fol. 125.

was much misliked by our puritans . . . And by that thesis he gott the ill will of all that tribe. Mr. Cotton of Boston sent him a letter about it blaming his medling & Dr. Ames another . . . he is a man thoroughly setled in his judgment for our Church in all things, and hath great friends amongst the States insomuch that there wilbe no doubt of him getting the 200 gilders per annum which Mr. Batchelor hopes to retaine: . . . Now I conceive his Majestie would like of this. . . . I know how Peters & that accusing tribe [of the Congregational classis] would be glad to find me medling about this. . . .[34]

However, Colonel Morgan would not accept Grim as his chaplain and, though Goffe complained that "Colonel Morgan in truth is the strangest man that I think lives" in as much as he refused both the English and the Dutch Reformed services, he admitted that Grim's "English Language is so imperfect that I doubt you it would please the officers." Goffe was finding the soldiers more tractable, for "wherein Last year I did all the work alone" in conducting public worship, "now with one accord & loud voice they all answer where in the Church of England they are wont to answer."[35] Morgan's chaplaincy was not filled for several months. Attempts were made to secure the appointment of John Forbes's son to the position, but Lord Vere could not approve, and a Mr. Gribbins served temporarily in Batchelor's place.[36]

By this time, too, the question of nonconformity in the English regiments had reached an impasse between English and Dutch authorities. In February, 1633, Stephen Goffe had collected information to prove that, until recently, the English liturgy had been regularly employed by the soldiers. The practice had been discarded largely because of the influence of the Congregational classis and those who went "the Forbesian way" in their services. Goffe found great diversity in the forms of service used in various garrisons:

In all the garrisons where they have no preacher [he wrote] the prayers are used. . . . It is to be observed that of those English Ministers which use not the English forme.

1. Some use the Dutch translated as Mr. Paine, but yet that mended, much left out, and somethings added, as may appear in Mr. Paine's booke.

2. Some use none at all, as Mr. Forbes, but everytime they administer

34 Goffe to Boswell, Wesel, May 5, 1633. *Boswell Papers*, I, fol. 134.
35 Goffe to Boswell, Rhynberg, May 15/25, 1633, in *Boswell Papers*, I, fol. 140.
36 Goffe to Boswell, Brussells, Aug. 19/29, 1633, in *ibid.*, I, fol. 152. Printed in Appendix XVII.

the sacraments a new [form]. They doe not stand to one yet their owne.
3. Some use another English forme putt out at Middleborough, 1586.
This Mr. Goodyear saith he useth at Leyden, and Mr. Peters said to me
that was the forme he found in his consistory. But whether he use it
or no I cannot tell. I believe he goes the Forbesian way.
4. Some use our English forme in the Sacraments, but mangle them
leaving out and putting in whole Sentences, And in Marriage, as Mr.
Balmford & Mr. Batchelor himselfe [did] at his garrison of Gorinchem.
And yet thinke they must not read a prayer or two at the beginning of
Service.[37]

Even Goffe, out of fear of becoming "very offensive to some,"
had shortened some of the prayers and prayed "the like in my
owne prayer before my Sermon."[38]   And as the Dutch were
about to become reconciled to the English use of the Anglican
forms among the soldiers, Dutch authorities were led to raise
up new objections.   Goffe reported it:

The quarrell now it seems is altered. It is not against prayers in a forme,
but against the contagion and perill of our books—That of Teachers
and Prophecying & the manner of ordaining of Elders which in this
book is different from the Dutch Church, and Mr. De Dieu [Dutch
professor at Leiden] tells me they have forbidden the two Last in their
churches that Elders should be ordained with Imposition of hands, and
their prophecyings. . . . But however neither Mr. Goodyear nor any
of the rest will say that this forme is enjoyned upon our nation here.[39]

Ambassador Boswell faithfully passed on to the Privy
Council all the data which his informants collected and, pending
definitive action, orders were given to all the colonels of the
English regiments in the Low Countries to employ none but
chaplains who conformed to the Church of England's service.[40]
By virtue of the protestations from the Congregational classis,
the Dutch authorities were highly troubled by these orders.
The Dutch Council of State reviewed the entire question before
the States General (March 25, 1633), stated they had referred
it to the theological faculty at Leiden who, in turn, had
recommended that this and similar disturbances among the
English could be avoided if the English churches would call

37 "Use of English Liturgy & Course of those who oppose the Church. 1633,"
   memorandum to Boswell in *Boswell Papers*, I, fol. 168. Published in part in
   Burrage, *Early English Dissenters*, I, 297-98.
38 Goffe to Boswell, Leiden, Feb. 12/22, 1632/33, in *Boswell Papers*, I, fol. 87.
39 Same to same, Leiden, Feb. 26, 1633, in *ibid.*, I, fol. 93.
40 *See*, besides the orders given to Vere, Morgan, and Herbert above, the memorial
   in *Boswell Papers*, I, fol. 98.

together their classis.[41]   Finally, on April 22, the States General resolved that English and Scottish preachers serving in Dutch cities should make no changes and bring in no innovations in their church services, but that, for the chaplains in the army, the Prince of Orange should see them properly disciplined.[42] This resolution gave the settled English ministers further opportunity to hide behind Dutch skirts in the stubborn practice of nonconformity; but the Prince of Orange hedged in an effort to avoid English displeasure and "said it was best men should practice according to the churches to which they belong"[43]—which neither opposed nor concurred in the English Privy Council's orders.   At this point, the matter rested in the early autumn of 1633.[44]   Until Ambassador Boswell and the Privy Council could enlist active Dutch co-operation, nothing further appeared to be possible in the way of bringing the chaplains to conformity.

IV.

No sooner did William Boswell begin his investigations of the Congregational classis than he encountered the fact that the classis legally rested, in part, upon express commission from the Dutch States.   Moreover, he discovered that, as the trouble between Misselden and Forbes had risen to such great heights that Dutch authorities heard of it, Forbes, Peter, and Balmford had been called before the Council of State and "asked why they did not execute their Commission granted (A.D. 1621) for keeping the English Ministers in better order?" The ministers replied "that they had been hindered by the

41 *Archief van de Staten-Generaal*: "Registers van ordinaris resolutien" (Dubbelen), No. 582 (1633), fol. 194 b.
42 *Ibid.* (Dubbelen), No. 582 (1633), fol. 265 b.   The States resolved ". . . goetgevonden ende verstaen datmen de saecke van d'Engelsche end Schotse predicanten bedienende in de steden van dese provincien eenige kercken bij provisie gelaten sal worden in soodanige staet als die tegenwoordich wert bevonden sonder eenige nieuwickeit oft ongebruijck toe te laten, ende wat belangt de saecke der predicanten heroupen tot bedieninge der Engelsche ofte Schotse regimenten int leger wert syne meer Hooch gemelte Ex*cie* versocht daerover een waeckent ooch te willen houden ende daer swaricheit soude mogen commen te outstaen daerover sulex te disponeren als deselve na syne hooge weysheit sal bevinden te behooren ende sal hierna ondertusschen werden gelesen ende geexamineert het voornoemde advis vanden meer welgemelte raet."
43 Goffe to Boswell, Rhynbergh, June 7, 1633.   *Boswell Papers*, I, fol. 144. Published in *Proceedings* of the Mass. Hist. Society, XLII, 221-22.
44 Troubles in the regiments still bothered Boswell, however.   See Goffe to Boswell, Brussels, Aug. 19/29, 1633, in Appendix XVII.

Belgic [Dutch Reformed] Churches, (2) opposed from England, (3) divided among themselves, (4) and not encouraged or assisted by their Lordships" of the Dutch Council.[45] Whereupon the Council had renewed their Commission of 1621 with warning that it

... shalbe by the preachers in the whole punctually observed and keapte, To the end that the English and Scottish preachers shall henceforward follow such *Classical order* as is held and followed in the *Walloon Churches* in this Country. Especially that good Care be taken on the quality, fitness, Life, Piety, opinion, doctrine, and Conversation of such as are admitted for preachers. And if it happens That any would make difficulty to obtaine the said orders, The said preachers shall instantly give notice thereof unto the said Councell to the ende to provide therein as it appartayneth.[46]

Thus, English and Dutch policies conflicted: the English hoping to crush the Congregational classis and prevent its allegedly unlawful functions, the Dutch giving sanction to its existence and urging it to extend its membership and activities in a manner wholly opposed by William Laud and the English Privy Council. However, there was one weakness in the classis's armor: it had been enjoined to keep order among the English and Scottish ministers in the Netherlands, a task almost impossible in view of the great divisions among them. If Boswell could demonstrate this inability of the classis to preserve ecclesiastical order, he would not only justify the Privy Council in rescinding King James's grant of 1621 but also he might be able to persuade the Dutch States General to withdraw their commission and agree to a new solution of the problems involved. Accordingly, the Ambassador turned loose his informers on the works of the classis and precipitated a thorough review of its legal foundations and activities in an effort to collect evidence to condemn it in Dutch as well as in English eyes.

In the course of 1633, William Boswell assembled wellsubstantiated materials to prove that the members of the Congregational classis, besides opposing the use of the Book of Common Prayer, conformed neither to English nor to Dutch

45 *See* Appendix XIV.
46 Translation of ''Act of the Council of State concerning the English & Scotch Ministers for holding Classical meetings &c. 28 Feb. 1633. At the Hague.'' *Boswell Papers*, I, fols. 94-95.

ecclesiastical orders, that, despite the orders of the English Privy Council, they arrogated to themselves the power of ordination, meddled with matters of creed and ceremony, published "scandalous" books and pamphlets, and concocted far-reaching plans to serve even further as a nursery for English nonconformity. Fortunately for Boswell, he did not have to depend solely upon accounts of past events for, in the course of 1633 alone, the Congregationalists furnished ample evidence of their nonconformity. For example, there was the case of Hugh Peter and the Rotterdam church. On March 29, 1632, Hugh Peter had gained permission of the City Council of Rotterdam to call a second preacher to be associated with him.[47] Dr. William Ames, who suffered severely from asthma, found the climate in Friesland injurious and was anxious to move. Evidently Ames had agreed with Peter that he was to go to Rotterdam for, on April 9, 1632, Peter's church reported to the Rotterdam Council that they had called the famous Doctor from the University of Franeker to be their second pastor.[48] The plan included the establishment at Rotterdam of a new Puritan college in which Ames was to be chief, if not only, instructor as well as assistant pastor of the church[49]—a scheme which must have made Laud's blood boil. Rotterdam authorities, however, approved highly, and they raised a sum of money for Ames equal to that which was paid Peter, six hundred gulden per year. Ames did not assume his new duties in Rotterdam until the summer of 1633, but when he arrived his scholarly reputation and learned presence lent great prestige to

---

47 Extract of the resolution of the Rotterdam City Council in Hugo Visscher, *Guilielmus Amesius* (Haarlem, 1894), 74 n. The plan had previously been approved by the States General but not with enthusiasm. When Peter proposed it, the States were discussing Misselden's case. Misselden had accused them of not suffering English subjects to be conformable to the Anglican Church. The States were in a bad mood and "whilest they were consulting on this business, Mr. Peter, preacher to the English Church at Rotterdam, coming to the States to make request unto them that Dr. Ames might be added for an assistant unto him, answere was made him by the States that he should keepe himselfe quiet, for that ere long they might par adventure have never an English preacher in the land, about which businesse they were now consulting, for as much as the Court at Delft sought an innovation in their land, which rather than they would suffer, they would soe farre from allowing two preachers in one towne, that haply there should be none at all suffered to preach in their dominions." "Afschriften der Depêches van de Nederlandsche Gezanten in Engeland aan de Staten-Generaal der Vereenigde Nederlanden. . . .," in *Add. MSS 17677 N*, fols. 317-18 (British Museum, London).
48 Visscher, *Amesius*, 74 n.
49 *Ibid.*, 74-75.

the Rotterdam church, to the newly intended college, and to the Congregational classis.

Early in 1633, before Ames's arrival and possibly in preparation for his coming, Hugh Peter remodelled the ecclesiastical structure of his church strictly upon the Congregational plan. He "gathered" his congregation anew, framed a covenant, and excluded from the sacraments all persons who refused to assent to the covenant. The covenant, like most Congregational covenants, was a very precise instrument. Alexander Browne procured for Boswell a copy of it which still remains in the latter's papers. Another copy, which Boswell sent to the Privy Council, is in the Public Record Office, London.[50] The Anglican authorities found it an amusing, though disloyal, document, but Peter was merely following orthodox Congregational practices. John Forbes, as president of the classis, presented the covenant to the Rotterdam congregation who voted, men and women alike, by a show of hands. Those who would not give assent were, in effect, excommunicated. Those who agreed to the covenant were then permitted to join together and "call" this minister anew. When this was done, Hugh Peter accepted the "call" and was ordained in his "new" charge by the laying on of hands by John Forbes and other members of the classis.

All this ceremony which appeared so piously proper to the participants was to William Boswell and his agents a seditious proceeding which asserted denial of the English church. When Alexander Browne sent a copy of the covenant to Boswell, he wrote,

I have here sent you Mr. Peters Covenant which he maide and unless wee will all subscribe to this his Covenant wee shall not be admitted to the lords Table neither old members nor newe: so that it seems to me our Church formerly was noe Church: but what authoritie he hath to doe these things, I know not; for he himselfe saith the Church of England doth tye the Conscience of men to do this and that, and he for his parte in this his Covenant Tieth both Conscience and parishioner.[51]

And Stephen Goffe wrote the story as it had been related to him,

50 *Boswell Papers*, I, fol. 161; *State Papers 16*, vol. 252, fol. 32. The covenant has often been published. See *Proceedings* of Mass. Hist. Society, XLII, 223-24; Rose-Troup, *John White*, Appendix II, 418-22; Burrage, *English Dissenters*, I, 302-303; II, 273-74; Hanbury, *Historical Memorials*, II, 309-10.

51 Browne to Boswell, Rotterdam, Nov. 1, 1633, in *Boswell Papers*, I, fol. 153. *See* footnote 21 above.

. . . 1. forsooth Mr. Peters would not be called by the vulgar English of Rotterdam, but by the Godly, & so he framed a NEW COVENANT in a paper to which they must putt their hands and none but those which were of that Covenant should have any voice to call him. That Covenant I cannot yet get a Copy of, but heare it was [a] pestilous precise thing by which tricke he did, as it were, Excommunicate 2 parts of the wonted congregation, they understanding no other new covenant but that of Christ in the Gospell. 2. Now the new Covenanters must come to the Election & confirmation of their Pastor: & in this work (said Mr. Forbes who then was president of the Classis, & preached the sermon) there are two parts χειροτονία & χειροθεσία, that you the people must do, this we the Presbytery. So, said he, expresse your election by holding up your hands. So the men held up their hands; but, said he, I see the men choose him, but what do the Women do? Hereupon the Women lift up their hands, too. 3. They came to the Imposition of hands, which was done by all the ministers present, Mr. Day only excepted, whose hands the Church of England had defiled; and thereupon his head STANDING lay their hands halfe an houre, all the which time Mr. Forbes with all the full fruition of his Episcopall office did pour upon him the burthen of his ministry. I need not comment upon this ridiculous & strange business: That which the Dutch disdaine, saying, it will make their discipline contemptible & that which we of England have reason to be greatly displeased with in as much as Peters was ordained before. . . . It is one of Mr. Forbes his propositions, That as one man can beget another so can one Minister ordaine another.[52]

As Browne's and Goffe's letters indicate, knowledge of these irregular proceedings was very displeasing to Boswell and the English Privy Council. Moreover, Boswell learned that the members of the classis took an important part in other distasteful practices. For instance, they were in constant communication with the most troublesome nonconformists in England in order to keep them advised of affairs in the Low Countries and themselves to keep abreast of the "progress of the reformation" in England.[53] Also, these men were active

52 Goffe to Gilbert Sheldon, *State Papers 16*, vol. 286, fol. 94 (P. R. O., London). The year in which this letter was written is not given. The *Cal. of State Papers, Dom. Ser., Chas. I, 1635*, lists it (28-29) as of 1635, but I am inclined, in the light of events taking place in Holland at the time, to place it in 1633. This letter has been printed in my ''Letters and Documents by or relating to Hugh Peter,'' in *Essex Institute Historical Collections*, LXXII, No. 1 (Jan., 1936), 47-49. I now believe I erred in dating it as of 1634. It is illuminating to compare Goffe's account of these ceremonies with Charles Gott's relation of the organization of the first church at Salem, Mass., in 1629, and the ordination of Higginson and Skelton there. See William Bradford, *History of Plimouth Plantation* (Boston, 1928), 316-17.

53 Evidences of this correspondence are preserved in *Collections* of the Mass. Hist. Society, 4th Series, VI, 10-12; VII, 14-16; *Winthrop Papers*, I, fol. 85 (MS in Mass. Hist. Society Library, Boston); *State Papers 16*, vol. 223, fol. 4

in writing and publishing books in Holland for Puritan edification in England. Forbidden editions of the Bible, catechisms,
treatises on ecclesiastical polity, and the like, especially by Ames
and Hooker, were secretly sent to England in great numbers.[54]
When William Ames's *A Fresh Suit Against Ceremonies*
appeared, Alexander Browne informed Boswell from Rotterdam that "there is a 100 or 200 bound at this towne to sell to
the good saintes which are in England." One Mr. Puckle,
"A Catterpillar to his Countrie as I may say," had the sale
of the books and his "chiefest uphoulder is Mr. Peter, that is
the truth."[55] A letter by Hugh Peter to Dr. Ames's brother-
in-law, the Reverend John Phillips of Wrentham, shows further
how deeply the Congregationalists in Holland were concerned
with the publication of books. This letter fell into the hands of
Laud to whom thanks are due for its preservation. The Bishop
endorsed it on the back:

Rec'd Aug. 30, 1633. This is a Copy of a Letter which I intercepted att
Yarmouth. The prototype was sent to Phillips (after my reading) by a
sailors boy. I had hoped to receive his Answer but the right Reverend
Phillips was too crafty.[56]

William Boswell, who became Sir William in July, 1633,
gave faithful accounts of these actions of the classis and its
members to the English Privy Council and ecclesiastical heads
in England.[57] As a whole, the accounts merely confirmed all
that Edward Misselden had reported to the Privy Council in
1632, and William Laud, who became Archbishop of Canterbury in August, 1633, was moved to decisive action. Already,
in March, 1633, Laud had offered a series of lengthy considerations to the Privy Council "concerning the dishonour done to

(P. R. O., London); *Transactions* of the Colonial Society of Mass., XIII, 60-69;
Rose-Troup, *John White*, 295-304; *Cal. of State Papers, Dom. Ser., Chas. I,
1633-34*, 113.

54 *Boswell Papers*, I, fols. 93, 123, 142, 178; *Collections* of the Mass. Hist.
Society, 4th Ser., VI, 4, 6; Cotton Mather, *Magnalia*, I, 226; Lawson, *William
Laud*, II, 284-86. Stephen Goffe rejoiced when William Ames died late in
1633, for it "hath putt us in hope that we shall not be troubled so much with
blue books as heretofore." *State Papers 16*, vol. 250, fol. 28 (P. R. O.)

55 Aug. 7/17, 1633, in *Boswell Papers*, I, fol. 150. Published in *Proceedings* of
the Mass. Hist. Society, XLII, 222. See also *Cal. of State Papers, Dom. Ser.,
Chas. I, 1633-34*, 213.

56 *Ibid.*, 113. Printed in full in John Browne, *History of Congregationalism . . .
of Norfolk and Suffolk* (London, 1877), 422-23.

57 Boswell to Bishop Williams, The Hague, May 8/18, 1633, in *Boswell Papers*,
I, fol. 136; *ibid.*, I, fol. 138, contains almost the same letter addressed to the
Lord Bishop of Durham.

the Church of England by the wilful negligence of some
Chaplains and other Ministers, both in our Factories and Regiments beyond the Seas." The core of the recommendations had
been that the Privy Council should command the English regiments and merchants in Holland to entertain none but ministers
who conformed in every particular to the Church of England;
and "That the *English* Ministers in *Holland,* being his Majesties born Subjects, be not suffered to hold any *Classical*
meetings, but howsoever not to assume the power of *Ordination;*
from which if they should not be restrained, there would be a
perpetual Seminary for breeding up men in Schism and Faction,
to the disturbance of this Kingdom."[58] Now, on October 1,
1633, the Privy Council, having debated Laud's proposals
against the background of Boswell's reports, "upon the voluntary Assent and submission of the said Company [of
Merchant Adventurers] not only of those here but of some
authorized of on the behalfe of those at Delft and Hamburg
now present before the Boards," resolved and ordered,

that they should not hereafter receave or admit of any Minister into
their said Churches in forreigne parts without his Majesties knowledge
and approbation of that person. And that the Liturgy and discipline now
used in the Church of England should bee receaved and established
there, And that in all things concerning their Church Government, they
should bee under the jurisdiction of the Lord Bishop of London as their
diocesan. For the orderly doing whereof Mr. Attorney Generall is
hereby prayed and required to advise and direct such a course as may
be most effectual.[59]

A short time later, in order to give effect to the Privy Council's
previous orders to the English troops, all English army chaplains
in foreign service were likewise brought under the ecclesiastical jurisdiction of the Bishop of London.[60] By these acts,
that freedom from English ecclesiastical authority which had
been one of the basic conditions underlying the formation of the
Congregational classis was removed. Given similar action by
Dutch authorities, the classis would be destroyed, conformity

58 Heylin, *Cyprianus Anglicus*, 218-20; Rushworth, *Historical Collections*, II, Part i,
   249-51.
59 Order of the King in Council, Oct. 1, 1633, in *State Papers 16*, vol. 247, fol. 2;
   briefed in *Cal. of State Papers, Dom. Ser., Chas. I, 1633-34*, 225; Heylin,
   Cyprianus, 269-60.
60 Heylin, *Cyprianus*, 259-60; Rushworth, *Historical Collections*, II, Part i, 249-51;
   Lawson, *William Laud*, II, 77.

would become enforceable, and Sir William's four-fold tasks would be accomplished.

V.

Boswell had the eager co-operation of English authorities in rescinding the action of James I which had clothed the classis with English approval. But it was a difficult and delicate matter to convince the Dutch authorities that their commission for the English classis should be withdrawn, especially as members of the classis had convinced many Dutch leaders that the Congregational classis was the only Dutch safeguard against popish innovations and unwarranted extension of the English church system into the Netherlands. To satisfy the Dutch that the Congregational classis was a dangerous, schismatical organization in their midst tried all of Sir William's diplomatic arts.

Various factors helped to bring the Dutch around to Boswell's point of view. One arose from the differences in opinion that existed among the Puritan ministers themselves. Not only did John Paget indignantly refuse to associate with the Congregational classis, and joined the Dutch synod instead, but Hugh Goodyear of Leiden rejected both polities, refused to be of any synod, denied communion to visiting persons of good repute, and generally appeared as a disorderly minister.[61] Moreover, the rigid discipline of the Congregationalists— which excommunicated persons held "ungodly" and not of the "elect"—caused such excommunicates to complain "of the difficulty of the way to Heaven here more than in England or the Gospell,"[62] and caused the English communities to be ecclesiastically disorderly in Dutch eyes. Of all these things, Dutch ecclesiastical authorities were made painfully aware by Boswell and his agents, especially by John Paget, who resented the Congregational classis's action in Hooker's case and its

61 Goffe to Boswell, Leiden, Dec. 13/23, *1633, Boswell Papers*, I, fol. 163. Printed in Appendix XVIII; *Cal. of State Papers, Dom. Ser., Chas. I, 1633-34*, 324. Goffe wrote to Boswell, Leiden, Feb. 12/22, 1632/33, that "*Mr. Goodyear* . . . refuseth to be of the *English Classis* which Mr. Forbes would establish, and is refused here amongst the Dutch. The reason is because they conceive him to be of a disagreeing disposition in generall, & in particular that he would governe his owne church with a more rigid discipline then is used or thought fitt by the Dutch Classis. . . ." *Boswell Papers*, I, fol. 87.
62 Goffe to Boswell, Leiden, Jan. 13/23, 1633/34, in *Boswell Papers*, I, fol. 179. Published in Burrage, *English Dissenters*, II, 284-85.

attempts to compel his association with them.   Accordingly,
Dutch ministers began to object to the English classis:

the two main reasons why the English Classis is condemned are these
(as they may be seene upon record) 1. Because the Ministers of England
which come over hither are of several & inconsistent opinions differing
from one another & from all reformed churches, as expressely that some
are Brownists, some Brownistically affected in particular opinions, as,
1. in allowing private men to preach. 2. In denying formes of praier. 3. In
admitting Brownists to their Congregations not renouncing their Brownisme.
Some are Jacobites who require a New Covenant for members of a church
to make before they can be communicants.   2. Condemne the Discipline
& Judging power of all Classes & Synods; & that they have only a power
of counsailing & advising, because every particular Congregation is a
church; and that a Compleat church, and that it is Immediately given
unto every Congregation from Christ to be a Single & uncompounded
policy; (These are the very words of Mr. Jacob, & Parker, & Baines.)
And now the Dutch Classis & Synods conclude that such opinions as these
do cleane overthrow the nature of their government; and that amongst
such diversity of opinion no true Classis can be framed.   2. Because of
the Complaint of the French & Wallons in those countries . . . because
they have a Classis graunted unto them: It were better (they say by
Experience) that they had no classis but were (as Mr. Paget is) mixed
into the Dutch Classis, for by reason of the distance of their dwelling
they cannot have Monthly or quarterly Meetings, as Classes have, but
only annuall as Synods: and that there is such trouble in their gathering
together some dwelling in one province & some in another at such great
distance that they never all meet & by reason of their few meetings
there grow up many Enormities in particular congregations unpunished. . . .

   That now in the this present yeare 1633, Mr. Forbes & his Classicks
obtaining a new Commission for their Classis from the Councell of
State, Mr. Paget hath presented the business againe to his classis at
Amsterdam the 4th of Aprill, being the first Monday in the month.
And they have promised their utmost endeavour to hinder it: that they
will press it to their Synod when it comes, & have delegates appoynted
to the States to declare the compleat judgement of their owne & divers
other classes & Synods against it.[63]

Stephen Goffe, upon his first visit to Amsterdam, discovered
Paget had secured even further action by Dutch ecclesiastical
authorities.   He reported as follows,

But the sport is that the puritans are at pittiful warres amongst themselves, those which will not have a classis (which are the best part)
against them which will have one.   And so Mr. Pagett, the Minister of

63 *Boswell Papers*, I, fol. 146. In Appendix IX. *See also Cal. of State Papers,
   Dom. Ser., Chas. I, 1633-34*, 30-31.

Amsterdam made me very welcome as thus far agreeing with him that I did oppose the English Classis, & so entertained me with many stories most necessary to be knowne.   One was Concerning the Classis what was done against it by the Dutch Ministers.   That he [Paget] being cited to be of it, he appealed to the Dutch Classis of Amsterdam, propounding to them his reasons [for refusing].   Who so affected the business, That they presently made an Act against it and caused it to be registered, with divers reasons whereof this was the chiefe: because the English Ministers which came over into these countries were of sundry opinions, some Brownisticall affected, some Jacobites, & some had wayes by themselves & so it would not be for the peace neither of Dutch nor English to give them a distinct body of government.   This was likewise concluded in the Utrecht Classis, and in Gelderland & at last in the North Holland Synod.   All which is to be taken notice that to see the perversions of these men that now seeke againe from the States to have their Act for a classis continued, when not only the King disallows it but the churches here.[64]

Thus, by the middle of 1633, Dutch ecclesiastical authorities had been brought to the conviction that the Congregational classis should be disallowed by the States.

However, Sir William Boswell and other enemies of the classis still needed to convince Dutch civil authorities.   And at this point, authorities in England took a hand.   For years, Dutch exiles in England driven thither by the Spanish Inquisition had been permitted to worship in their own fashion without English interference.   Now, in January, 1634, Archbishop Laud reported to the Privy Council,

I conceive under favour that the Dutch Churches in Canterbury & Sandwich are great Nurseryes of Inconformity in those Partes.   Your Majesty may be pleased to remember I have complained to your selfe and my Lords at the Counsell Board & humbly desired that they both of the French, Italian, & Dutch Congregations, which are borne Subjects, may not be suffered any longer to live in such Separation as they doe from both Church and State.   And have accordingly . . . commanded my

---

64 *See* footnote 52 above. *Cf.* also Goffe to Edward Misselden, Wesel, April 26, 1633 (o.s.), in *State Papers 16*, vol. 237, fol. 48 (P.R.O.).   Briefed in *Cal. of State Papers, Dom. Ser., Chas, I, 1633-34*, 30, and published in part in *Proceedings* of Mass. Hist. Society, XLII, 216.   Goffe wrote: "But Mr. Pagett saith he hath first gott an Act from the Amsterdam Classis & then from the North-Holland Synod, then from theire Classis of Utrecht upon certaine Reasons which he putt in against the English Classis, That in theire opinions it is not safe for the Dutch Churches to permitt the English to have a Classis.   The reasons given in and registered are many, this one, because the men who sue for a Classis are such who have Schismaticall self-opinions wherein they differ both from the Church of England and the Dutch and all other Reformed Churches."

Vicar Generall . . . to beginn fairely to call them to conforme with the English Church.[65]

Later (December 19, 1634), the Archbishop, ignoring appeals from the Dutch residents and Dutch authorities, gave orders that all English born members of these foreign congregations must conform to the English church by March 15, 1635. This order created a great stir. Some one hundred forty Dutch families removed to Holland and the Dutch States protested against English severity. But the Privy Council replied that unless the States General withdrew its support of the Congregational classis and permitted English subjects to conform to the English church in the Netherlands, the Dutch churches in England would be compelled to conform wholly to the Anglican church.[66]

Simultaneously, the Privy Council brought another diplomatic force to bear upon the Dutch. In order to save money in Charles I's depleted treasury, the English government cut down the quantities of war materials and the number of soldiers sent to Holland to support the Dutch in their war with Spain. Doubtless the measure was occasioned largely by internal English financial circumstances, but it had diplomatic value as well. Stephen Goffe reported its effect to the Privy Council:

The denying of supplies of Soldiers out of England hath beene a very good thing for the prosperity of our church, for now the States themselves & our Duchified Captaines, & the professors of Leyden all say that they have no reason to displease the king in hindering him from governing his owne people after his owne Lawes. And they think that their opposing of the order of the Church hath beene one cause of the restraint.[67]

But the case that finally prompted the States General to act was precipitated by the Congregational classis itself. This

65 "My Lord Archbishop of Canterbury his Certificat upon his Majesties Instructions," Jan. 2, 1634. In *Harleian MSS 787*, fol. 32 (B. M., London); *Cal. of State Papers, Dom. Ser., Chas. I, 1633-34*, 556-57; Lawson, *William Laud*, II, 77-86.

66 *Ibid.;* David Macpherson, *Annals of Commerce* (4 vols., London, 1805), II, 382; Rushworth, *Historical Collections*, II, Part i, 272-73; *Cal. of State Papers, Dom. Ser., Chas. I, 1634-35*, 340-41, 380; "Afschriften der Depêches . . .," in *Add. MSS 17677 N*, fols. 317-18; *ibid.*, in *Add. MSS 17677 O*, fols. 281-86, 301-305 (B.M., London).

67 Goffe to ?, The Hague, Nov. 7/17, 1633, in *State Papers 16*, vol. 250, fol. 28; briefed in *Cal. of State Papers, Dom. Ser., Chas. I, 1633/34*, 279-80. *Cf.* also *Archief van de Staten-Generaal*: "Registers van Ordinaris resolutien" (1634), No. 583, Dubbelen, fols. 100, 100b, 421, 428 (The Hague, Holland).

case, quite similar to that of Thomas Hooker a short time before, grew out of John Davenport's migration to Holland late in 1633. Like Hooker, Davenport was a prominent nonconformist in England. As early as 1624, the Bishop of London had suspected him of nonconformity. Through the intercession of Lord Conway, to whom he applied for aid, Davenport escaped being silenced at that time.[68] During most of the next decade, Davenport preached at St. Stephen's Church in Coleman Street, London. Late in the autumn of 1633, strongly suspected of irregularity by the Bishop of London and evidently fearing imprisonment for his rôle as one of the feoffees in the impropriations scheme, Davenport fled to Holland in decidedly suspicious circumstances. Stephen Goffe described his arrival as follows:

> We have another Bishop come, who will take it ill if we have not more than absolute primacy. And to be short, It is Mr. Davenport, who landed here about a moneth agoe. He came over in one Humphrey his shipp, by the conduct and contrivance of Mr. Stone, a merchant in Coleman Street. He was disguised in a gray suite, & an overgrowne beard, and at his landing was presently with his accomplices put a horseback and before all were wel landed was gott to Rotterdam, where they had a supper (Peter being there to make uses), and all the discourse was the Wonderful providence of God. His errand was to Amsterdam to be chosen Minister there. There he hath preached twice every Sunday since he came.[69]

Davenport denied that he had left England in disguise or ill favor of the Bishop of London, lest the English ecclesiastical authority so recently extended to Holland be invoked against him. He protested to Boswell that he had left England for a rest of a few months, that malicious persons in Holland had reported such slanderous things of him that his return was "made much more difficult and hazardous than I could suspect."[70] It is clear, however, that Davenport had fled from England to escape persecution.[71]

Moreover, it is clear that Davenport left England in re-

68 ''Conway Papers,'' in *State Papers 14*, vol. 173, fols. 42, 43, 44, 51 (P.R.O., London). Isabel B. Calder (ed.), *Letters of John Davenport* (New Haven, 1937), 13 ff.
69 Goffe to William Brough, The Hague, Dec. 16/26, 1633, *State Papers 16*, vol. 252, fol. 55. *Cf. Cal. of State Papers, Dom. Ser., Chas. I, 1633-34*, 324.
70 Davenport to Boswell, Amsterdam, March 18, 1634 (n.s.), in *Boswell Papers*, I, fol. 196; published in Calder, *John Davenport*, 40-43.
71 Laud reproached him in the Court of High Commission soon after his departure. See *ibid*.

sponse to a call from the English church in Amsterdam.[72]
Stephen Oswood and the Congregationally-minded group in
John Paget's church (the same that had been balked in choosing
Hooker[73]), taking advantage of the illness of the aged Mr.
Paget, had issued a "call" to Davenport to become co-pastor
of their church.[74] As in Hooker's case, the "call" was irregular, subject to the approval of the magistrates and the Dutch
classis of Amsterdam, and Stephen Goffe made haste to inform Paget and the Dutch officials that Davenport was likely
to be of the same breed of schismatic as Hooker had been;
"knowing the story of Mr. Hooker," Goffe warned Paget

what a colleague he was like to have. After much welcome discourse
unto him he made me this promise that what questions were proposed
to Mr. Hooker the very same he [Davenport] should undergoe. And
that he must be of the Dutch Classis, which the Forbesian & precise
puritans abhor as much as our discipline, and that he could not be
chosen without the consent of the Magistrates. Hereupon (when I heard
mention of the Magistrates) I went unto Mr. Vossius and acquainted
him with the business, which he took notes of in a paper for his memory.[75]

Unlike Hooker, however, Davenport, with some hesitation,
appeared at first to be willing to join the Dutch classis, and
the matter of his election passed to the magistrates. The
latter, too, were about to approve, when Vossius objected upon
the basis of the information supplied him by Goffe, to the
effect that Davenport had fled from England for nonconformity; that he opposed the Dutch Reformed Church even as
he did the English; that he preached against civil government;
that he was of the same stamp with Hooker "who their owne
Dutch Ministers thought incapable of being a minister in their
church. That because it was likely he held the same opinions
it was fitt he should be tried by the same questions by which
he was";[76] and that if a man be sent over from England to
tell Davenport's

manner of forsaking his King & Church, & his obnoxiousness unto the
King for other matters, & that he was not particularly questioned for

72 Boswell knew of it before his arrival. See Boswell to Secretary John Coke,
    The Hague, Nov. 4, 1633. In *Boswell Papers*, I, fols. 154-56.
73 See above, Chapter II, 27 ff.
74 Goffe to Boswell, Amsterdam, Feb. 15/25, 1633/34, in *Boswell Papers*, I, fol.
    188. Printed in *Proceedings* of Mass. Hist. Society, XLII, 225.
75 Goffe to William Brough, The Hague, Dec. 16/26, 1633, in *State Papers 16*,
    vol. 252, fol. 55 (P.R.O.).
76 Goffe to William Brough, The Hague, Dec. 16/26, 1633, in *State Papers 16*, vol.
    252, fol. 55 (P.R.O.).

church discipline, then I doubt not but we shalbe delivered from this plague too, & He will make for New England whither Mr. Cotton & his Sonne borne a shipboard & so called Sea-borne, & Mr. Hooker are safely arrived, (as they say here) by Speciall, Extraordinary prosperous winds.[77]

And thus, by such arguments as these, Vossius stayed Davenport's election by the magistrates pending further examination of the case.

At this point, Davenport and his Amsterdam friends appealed to the Congregational classis for support and the issue became joined, with John Forbes, Hugh Peter, and the Congregational classis on the one hand, and John Paget, William Boswell, and Stephen Goffe on the other, bombarding the perplexed magistrates with highly colored accounts, *pro* and *con,* of Davenport's orthodoxy, motives, and abilities. For a time, it appeared as though the Congregationalists would win. Davenport's reputation was great, his supporters numerous and anxious for his election. Moreover, the Dutch still harbored suspicions which the Congregationalists were careful to inflame to the effect that the English government extended ecclesiastical control not only to discipline their own subjects in Holland but also to gain "some intended power over the Dutch themselves."[78] But the point that stuck in the magistrates' minds was Goffe's charge that Davenport was a fugitive from English justice. In view of the recent English orders of the King in Council, the Dutch courted no trouble by harboring runaway English sectaries. Thus, despite Congregational wooing, the magistrates held back and permitted John Paget to confront Davenport with the same "20 Propositions" with which he had previously baited Thomas Hooker. Davenport's replies indicated that he still appeared willing to join the Dutch classis, but uncertainty arose over his reply to the sixth "Proposition," which read: "Whether Infants whose Parents are not Members of the Church may be lawfully baptized according to the manner of the Reformed Churches." Davenport took exception to "the unlimited Baptising of all infants," but agreed to baptize children of non-members if he be permitted to give "a precise examination" to prove that "they are Christians in

77 Goffe to Gilbert Sheldon, Leiden, Feb. 3/13, 1633/34, in *State Papers 16,* vol. 260, fol. 13.
78 Goffe to Boswell, Leiden, Jan. 7, 1634. *Boswell Papers,* I, fol. 176.

deed."[79]   Paget was dissatisfied with the response and took Davenport's answers to five Dutch ministers who objected to Davenport's "precise examination" in some cases and, as Davenport said, took "the word Christian more largely than I, for they account all Christians which professe Christian religion. . . ."[80] Over this point the issue dragged for months. Davenport and his friends protested to the Dutch against Paget "for his difficulty in admitting so reverent a colleague &c," but the Dutch ministers, after consulting Paget, "concluded that a more Sollemne meeting Should be had & Davenport perswaded to a better sense or els no admission." Accordingly a meeting was held and the Dutch divines wrote in Latin the conditions they required of Davenport, to this effect:

That if the Parent or frends of the infant did signifie unto him before hand that they would have a child baptized, That then Mr. Pagett should send them to Davenport to be examined as he desired. On Davenport's part, That if the Parent or frends being desired to go to him should not go or, coming, should be so ignorant as not to be able to give account of their faith, or if they should suddainly bring the child into the Church without forewarning that he should not venture to refuse to baptize it.

Both the Dutch classis and the magistrates agreed to accept Davenport on these conditions, but Davenport procrastinated and, after a delay of several weeks, refused, saying "That he could not with a good Conscience perform them."[81]   This refusal offended the Dutch ministers, although they agreed to hear Davenport's "grievances." But when the latter requested that Forbes and Peter be permitted to accompany him to the Dutch classis's meeting, the Dutch refused, gave Davenport until the first Monday in May (1634) to give his final word to the conditions of the five ministers. According to Goffe,

This hath cost Forbes & Peters and Batchellor another jorney to Amsterdam, who have (as they phrase it) Strengthened him, & Mr. Batchelor told me himselfe that Mr. Davenport will not nor cannot yield unto their Classis and that he is resolved not to stay; and they Speake it in praise of Mr. Peters Courage & Zeale that he should often use this speech to Mr. Davenport: 'Take heed, Mr. D., what you do,

79 See Davenport's *A True Report of Passages Betweene Mr. Paget and Me In This Business*, published in *Proceedings* of the Mass. Hist. Society, XLIII, 49; *Cal. of State Papers, Dom. Ser., Chas. I, 1635-36*, 48; Calder, *John Davenport*, 43-55.
80 *Ibid.*, 51-52; cf. also *Cal. of State Papers, Dom. Ser., Chas. I, 1634-35*, 469; Hanbury, *Memorials*, I, 537.
81 *Boswell Papers*, I, fol. 192, in Burrage, *Early English Dissenters*, II, 278-80.

for you were as good yeeld to the English Bishops as to the Dutch Classis.'[82]

Meanwhile, as the case dragged on, a series of incidents heightened the controversy. Goffe and Boswell sought to discover the exact circumstances of Davenport's departure from England. Davenport confessed that he would not have come to Holland if he had "bene secure of a safe and quiett abode in my deare native Country," but he denied having preached or written against the civil authorities either of England or of the Netherlands.[83] Davenport's friends in the Congregational classis and in Amsterdam exasperated Paget and his Dutch colleagues by bitter accusations against the former and multitudinous appeals to the latter. In March, 1634, when Davenport appeared to refuse the conditions regarding baptism, a delegation begged the Dutch classis, "in the name of the *most & Choicest* of the Congregation," to admit Davenport "not Pastor but Assistant in preaching" but the classis refused, saying "To that matter of being Lecturer or assistant in preaching only, that was a Species of Creature which was not in their Church."[84] Furthermore, so impatient were Davenport's admirers that, pending the outcome of the disputes, they prevailed upon him to preach to "the *most* and *Choicest* of the Congregation" as a "gathered congregation" in a private house in Amsterdam. This unfortunate business proved to Dutch authorities that Davenport was a wilful and dangerous schismatic such as the King of England had proclaimed against in the preceding autumn. Consequently, as one of Boswell's informers wrote in April, 1634:

Mr. Davenport is still a Nonconformist to the Dutch Churches as well as to the English in many points . . . and (whatsoever the issue of his suite may be) it is manifeste that the Dutch ministers doe mislike our Nonconformists and would more Easilie entertaine Conformable men of Learning and good life and moderation. Now they doe now profess at Amsterdam that they will not continue the stipend to any English minister who comes against the King of Englands pleasure.[85]

82 Goffe to Boswell, The Hague, April 7/17, 1634. *Boswell Papers*, I, fol. 198. Published in *Proceedings* of the Mass. Hist. Society, XLII, 230-31.

83 *Boswell Papers*, I, fols. 178, 188, 196; Burrage, *English Dissenters*, II, 282-84; Calder, *John Davenport*, 40-43.

84 Goffe to Boswell, Leiden, March 9, 1634. *Boswell Papers*, I, fol. 194. Published in Burrage, *English Dissenters*, II, 281-82.

85 Dr. Griffin Higgs to Boswell, The Hague, April 9, 1634. *Boswell Papers*, I, fol. 200. Published in Burrage, *English Dissenters*, II, 285-86, and in *Proceedings* of the Mass. Hist. Society, XLII, 232.

It appears likely, then, that even if Davenport had accepted the conditions stipulated by the Dutch classis, the Dutch ministers and magistrates had become so unfavorable that they would not have tolerated him in the Amsterdam church.

However, Davenport not only refused the conditions with reference to the baptism of infants but, in orthodox Congregational fashion, he denied the ruling authority of the Dutch classis as well.[86] After this, both Boswell and Dutch authorities strove to prevent Davenport from preaching anywhere in the Netherlands; and Davenport and his supporters engaged in a long and bitter pamphlet controversy with John Paget over the question of the baptism of the non-elect.[87] Paget was accused of nursing a perverse spirit which led him to the "Continual opposition to the truth" and to disgrace "the most deare Servants of God." John Tracy of the Amsterdam church wrote him,

Doe not think that your pretense of error will ever excuse you for your opposition of all men of eminentcy that have beene either nominated or chosen to this place; for unless greater differences than those be borne with love, never two men of eminentcy can live in peace together if their Consciences be Cleare & tender. Mr. Parker, good man, he was not for your tune; Mr. Peters you desired but would not contend for, if any dare beleeve it; Mr. Ames, Mr. Forbes, Mr. Hooker, Mr. Davenport doe all hold errors, & I beleeve there is not an eminent man in the world but if he were nominated or Chosen to be here, you would find some error in him to keep him out. . . .[88]

Paget's was indeed a remarkable record for one who himself was an English refugee in Holland for conscience's sake. Meanwhile, Davenport, hounded by Dutch authorities, preached secretly for a time in Amsterdam, assisted Hugh Peter for a few months at Rotterdam,[89] and finally, returning to England early in 1635, he gathered his loyal friends together and sailed for New England in 1637.

John Davenport's case had repeatedly drawn the unfavorable attention of Dutch officials, both civil and ecclesiastical, not only to Davenport himself but also to the Congregational

86 Hanbury, *Memorials*, I, 642; Burrage, *English Dissenters*, I, 306-309.
87 The chief tracts of this controversy are published in the *Proceedings* of the Mass. Hist. Society, XLIII, 45-68.
88 John Tracy to John Paget, Amsterdam, Sept. 9, 1634. *Add. MSS 24, 666*, fols. 1-3 (B. M.). For another letter by Tracy see Appendix XIX.
89 His son, John, Jr., was baptized there, April 15, 1635. *See* Steven, *The Scottish Church, Rotterdam*, 310 n.

classis which had supported him in his stubborn nonconformity. And just as the Dutch classis in Amsterdam and elsewhere, together with the South Holland Synod, had reached the conclusion that it was undesirable and dangerous to the Dutch Reformed churches for the English ministers to be permitted to maintain an independent classis of their own, so the magistrates in Amsterdam and, finally, the Dutch Council of State came to the same opinion. Dutch official realization that the Congregationalists never could effect that order among English ministers for which their classis had been instituted, and that they had never intended to conform to the Dutch Reformed Church as had been hoped, stilled Dutch opposition to English attempts to extend prelatical control over the chaplains and English congregations in the Netherlands. Moreover, the Dutch Council of State, without rescinding its commission to the Congregational classis, took action that was fully as effective and pleasing in the sight of Sir William Boswell. Early in March, 1634, before Davenport's case was settled, the Council, taking note of the disorders among the English and Scottish ministers to the "Scandall of the Congregations and disservice of the Lande," issued warning that "the order taken or made the xxviith of December, 1621 [by which the Dutch had given legal constitution to the Congregational classis] shalbe by the preachers in the whole punctually observed and keapte." Moreover, the Council went on to interpret that act according to its original intent, namely, that the English and Scottish ministers were to conform to the "classical order" of the Dutch Reformed Church.[90] By this specific interpretation, the Congregational classis had, in fact, lost its last legal prop. Sir William Boswell's fourfold task was completed: John Forbes had been ousted from Delft,[91] an Anglican was installed in his place, and the church was reduced to stubborn conformity; chaplains in the English troops and ministers to

90 *Boswell Papers*, I, fols. 94-95, 98. Samuel Balmford to the Archbishop of Canterbury, London, Sept. 30, 1635 (o. s.), in *Add. MSS 17677 O*, fols. 409 b-411 (British Museum); Albert Joachimi to the States General, London, March 27, 1635, in *ibid.*, fols. 301-305.

91 The salutary effect of the Dutch action is seen in the fact reported by his son that John Forbes, being in Amsterdam in April, 1634, at the time Davenport's case was still hotly argued, "would not meddle in the business, fearing at last they will break their church in pieces by division." *See* James Forbes to Dr. John Stoughton, Delft, April 8, 1634, in *Cal. of State Papers, Dom. Ser., Chas. I, 1633-34*, 545.

the Merchant Adventurers had been brought under the diocese of London with Dutch consent; the Congregational classis had been deprived of its English legal recognition, compelled to conform to Dutch ecclesiastical order or dissolve; and the Dutch government had been brought to a decidedly hostile attitude towards English refugees for nonconformity in Holland.

CHAPTER V

DISSOLUTION OF THE CLASSIS—AND LATER

I.

Because of the steps taken by the English Privy Council late in 1633 and by the Dutch Council of State early in 1634, all English and Scottish ministers in the Dutch Netherlands who held charges either with the English troops or with the Merchant Adventurers were compelled to conform either to the Church of England as of the diocese of London or to the Dutch Reformed Church subject to the discipline of synods regularly constituted under Dutch authority. The consciences of true Congregationalists permitted neither choice. Their last hope was to seek refuge afresh in the New World towards which their eyes already had been anxiously directed by the experiments in the Massachusetts Bay and in Old Providence Isle. Thomas Hooker had migrated to New England in 1633. William Ames had intended to go if his Rotterdam projects failed, but he died in November, 1633, before their inevitable failure became apparent. John Forbes, finally ousted from his church at Delft in January, 1634, toyed with the notion of migrating to New England and died in the summer of 1634, before he had come to a decision. John Davenport returned to England in 1635 and arrived in New England two years later. Hugh Peter gave up his charge at Rotterdam in 1635, and accepted a call to become Roger Williams's successor at Salem, Massachusetts. Samuel Balmford may possibly have intended to go to New England, but when he returned to England in 1635 he was seized by a pursuivant of Laud's Court of High Commission, detained, and finally rescued only by Dutch intercession because he plead, as a Dutch paid minister of The Hague, that he was subject to the government of Holland and to the Dutch classis at The Hague.[1] And Cotton Mather relates that when John Cotton was silenced at Boston

---

1 See Balmford's letter to Archbishop Laud, London, Sept. 23, 1635 (o.s.), in *Add. MSS 17677 O*, fols. 409-b-411 (British Museum).

in 1633, he had intended to join the Congregationalists in Holland but was informed by Hooker of the increasingly tense situation there and determined to go to New England instead.[2] By 1635, then, the Congregational classis had been effectually dissolved by the death or migration of its leaders, and knowledge of its fate—or impending fate—had deflected from Holland to New England a substantial number of the most prominent early leaders in the New England colonies. A curious conjunction of Congregational disasters made New England their last and only refuge: hopes in Parliament, in the feoffees for purchase of impropriations, and in the Congregational classis in Holland had failed to make possible in the Old World the realization of "Discipline out of the Word" as Congregationalists understood it.

Before the year 1635 closed, the Dutch Netherlands became even less possible as a place of refuge for English Congregationalists. Archbishop Laud's vigorous exertions brought foreign chaplaincies under jurisdiction of the Bishop of London. Many of the Puritan officers who had patronized nonconformist preachers were removed from the army; and Stephen Goffe saw to it that the army chaplains were Church of England men. Moreover, following Edward Misselden's proposed "Remedies" of 1632, the Privy Council interfered in the government of the Company of Merchant Adventurers. In 1635, the Court of the Merchants at Hamburg was reduced to subserviency to the Court at London, the merchants' factory at Delft was abolished, and a new one was established at Rotterdam with a monopoly of the woollen trade in the Low Countries.[3] That the new Court was severely opposed to nonconformists is demonstrated by the following document transmitted to the English Privy Council by the Company's Court at London. As woollen trade was concentrated at Rotterdam, English merchants at Amsterdam appealed to those at Delft to be admitted into their fellowship,

so as those of them who had married foreign-born women might not be caused to remove themselves with their families into England according to

2 *Magnalia Christi Americana*, I, 241-42.

3 "Afschriften der Depêches . . . 1633-1635," in *Add. MSS 17677 O*, fols. 301-305; *Calendar of State Papers, Domestic Series, Charles I, 1635-36*, 34-36; C. Te Lintum, *De Merchant Adventurers in De Nederlanden* (The Hague, 1905), 105 ff.

the ancient charter of the Merchant Adventurers, and that such of them as had joined with the English Church of separation there, might be permitted to have the freedom of their consciences in matters of religion. These propositions being sent over to the Merchant Adventurers here, their answer was that those who had married abroad must, according to the charters, remove with their families into England within such time as the company there should limit, which was usually about four years; and as to the second point, that whosoever would be of their fellowship must be of the Church of England.[4]

II.

The dissolution of the Congregational classis and other changes effected by the English government did not immediately quiet all nonconformity in the Dutch Netherlands. George Beaumont, who succeeded John Forbes at Delft and later moved with the merchants to Rotterdam, had constant trouble with his congregation, many members of which refused to attend his services; and Beaumont soon relinquished the charge.[5] John Forbes's son, Patrick, caused great disturbance at Delft, in the army, and elsewhere. Some of the English merchants at Delft severed their connection with the Company of Merchant Adventurers and did not move to Rotterdam. Early in 1636, they obtained provisional permission from the Delft magistrates to open a church of their own, without application to the Dutch church council at Delft. The church gathered and called Patrick Forbes as its minister. When the church council investigated and inquired "whether they intended to conforme themselves to the order of the Church of England or . . . to the order of the Netherlandish Church . . .," they replied "they had rather conforme themselves to the order of the Netherlandish Church."[6] But, in the meantime, Forbes attracted unfavorable attention by a particularly "rayling Sermon" which prompted the Delft magistrates to investigate. Whereupon, Forbes disappeared and, as the entire proceedings

4 *Cal. of State Papers, Dom. Ser., Chas. I, 1635-36*, 36.
5 Edward Misselden to Secretary Windebank, Hackney, June 26, 1635, in *State Papers 16*, vol. 291, fol. 71 (P.R.O., London). Briefed in *Cal. of State Papers, Dom. Ser., Chas. I, 1635*, 151; Misselden to Boswell, Hackney, April 28, 1637, in *Boswell Papers*, I, fol. 255; George Beaumont to Boswell, Rotterdam, Dec. 28, 1635, and March 30, 1636, in *ibid.*, I, fols. 213, 232; Goffe to Boswell, Oatlands, Oct. 5, 1636, in *ibid.*, I, fol. 247; Beaumont to Archbishop Laud, Rotterdam, March 14, 1635/36, in *Cal. of State Papers, Dom. Ser., Chas. I, 1635-36*, 295.
6 J. C. Flexham to William Boswell, Delft, March 7, 1636, in *Boswell Papers*, I, fol. 224. See also the extracts of Flexham's earlier letter in Appendix XX.

had been irregular, the congregation was refused separate maintenance for a minister and a church.[7]   Later, in 1638, young Forbes became chaplain in a Scottish regiment at Breda and necessitated further disciplining by opposing the use of the English Book of Common Prayer, as Samuel Batchelor had done years before.[8]

Furthermore, Congregationalists still remained in the English churches at Rotterdam, Amsterdam, and elsewhere who, whenever possible, called a minister of their own persuasion.   Archbishop Laud's "policy of thorough" furnished them with numerous candidates.   Philip Nye quietly assumed the pastorate of a small church at Arnheim in 1633, where later Thomas Goodwin also found refuge; Jeremiah Burroughs, John Ward, William Bridge, and Sidrach Simpson established themselves at Rotterdam for a time after 1636.   All these men had been required to leave England because of nonconformity. Evidently their congregations consisted of English merchants and others who no longer were associated with the Merchant Adventurers (or never had been), were therefore not so directly subject to English ecclesiastical control, and were tolerated in small numbers by the Dutch authorities who hoped, through them, to discover closely guarded secrets of the English staple trade.[9]   Moreover, this new generation of Congregationalists were less noisy than the Forbesian group had been, they made no attempt to interfere with the forms of worship employed among the English soldiers or the English Company

7 Same to same, Delft, March 12, 1636, in *ibid.*, fols. 226-27.
8 See letters of Goffe to Boswell, Breda, Nov. 21, Dec. ?, 1637; and Richard Dell to Boswell, Breda, Jan. 11, 20; June 12, 1638.   All in *Boswell Papers*, I, fols. 264, 268, 279, 295, 300-301 respectively.
9 This later group established in Rotterdam was closely associated with the Congregational churches at Norwich, Great Yarmouth, and vicinity in England. In 1640, many of them returned to England: ''But after the glad tidings of a hopefull Parliament called & convened in England was reported to the Church aforesayd in Rotterdam, divers of the Church whose hearts God stirred up to further the light (they now saw) by all lawfull meanes in their native Country not without hope of injoying liberty there.''   After conference with their brethren in Rotterdam, ''and seeking God for direction, they returned, with the assent, approbation, and prayers of the Church, into England with resolution to gather a church with all convenient speed . . .''   William Bridge returned and became their pastor.   See Joseph Davey, ''The Church at Great Yarmouth during the Commonwealth,'' *Harmer MSS No. 3*, in Dr. Williams's Library, London, fol. 73 ff.; also Davey, ''The Entire Records of the Congregational Church at Great Yarmouth from its foundation in 1642 to . . . 1813.   Copied from the Church Book . . . ,'' *Harmer MSS No. 2*, Dr. Williams's Library, 1 ff.

of Merchant Adventurers, and they had no independently organized classis with which to exercise ecclesiastical pressure on
their fellows.   Charles I, Laud, and the Privy Council, having
more pressing problems of finance and conformity on their
hands at home, gave them little attention, although Laud, as a
safeguard, "so effectually managed matters by means of the
Ambassador at The Hague that a proclamation was issued by
the States General of the Provinces [in 1638] against those
who published seditious and libellous books against the Church
of England and the government of the kingdom."[10]

III.

To Congregationalists, the enforced dissolution of their
classis in the Dutch Netherlands was an important event. It
not only effectually closed the Netherlands as a place of refuge
for English nonconformists who desired to erect the "Congregational way" in their churches without interference; it also
demonstrated the perfidy of the English prelatical system, and
particularly of Archbishop Laud, who would not wash his
hands of English nonconformists wheresoever they might flee.
For if the Archbishop extended English ecclesiastical authority
over English refugees and others in Holland, what was to
prevent a similar extension of prelatical power to the Massachusetts Bay Colony?[11]   Moreover, the embittered relations of
the Congregational classis with John Paget and the Presbyterian system publicly emphasized, probably for the first time,
the differences between Congregationalists and Presbyterians—
differences that became more and more evident as the Long
Parliament, the Westminster Assembly, and the English Civil
Wars brought the two ecclesiastical systems into violent competition.   And John Milton's classic line "On the New Forces
of Conscience under the Long Parliament," to the effect that
"New Presbyter is but old Priest writ large," was but a
corroborative echo of Hugh Peter's warning in 1634, "Take
heed, Mr. D., what you do, for you were as good yeeld to the
English Bishops as to the Dutch Classis."   All the pious efforts

10 Lawson, *William Laud*, II, 286.
11 This fear in the hearts of New World Congregationalists is clearly shown
   in a letter from Roger Wood, Governor of the Bermudas, to Dr. William Ames.
   See G. L. Kittredge, "A Note on Dr. William Ames," *Transactions* of the
   Colonial Society of Mass., XIII, 60-69.

of John Dury, Richard Baxter, and a host of others failed to unite the two sects which here, in the Dutch Netherlands, first discovered, in miniature, the enormity of their ecclesiastical differences.

Finally, the temporarily full expression of the Congregational ecclesiastical polity in Holland had its reverberations in the New World. Not only did the dissolution of the classis provide the immediate cause for the emigration of several of the most outstanding ministers to New England, but the first hand knowledge of the Dutch nation and, to some degree, of the Dutch tongue which Hooker, Davenport, and Peter had gained was of value to the New England colonies. Hugh Peter employed his Dutch contacts for the purchase of supplies for the Bay Colony,[12] and the Connecticut leaders' first-hand knowledge of the Dutch may have assisted them to maintain friendly relations with New Amsterdam despite angry commercial competition and knotty boundary problems. Either by accident or by design, some of the civil institutions of the New England colonies were patterned after those of the Dutch,[13] and the military lessons of the Dutch Wars, especially as learned by Lyon Gardiner and Captain John Underhill, were not lost upon the English colonists.[14] Thus, tempered and matured by Dutch experience, the holy crusade to realize "Discipline out of the Word" as Congregationalists understood it found liberty of free expression in the wildernesses of the New World.

12 N. B. Shurtleff (ed.), *Records of the Governor and Company of the Massachusetts Bay* (5 vols., Boston, 1853-54), I, 259.
13 Douglas Campbell, *The Puritan in Holland, England, and America* (N. Y., 1892), *passim.*
14 See the sketches of Gardiner and Underhill in the *Dictionary of American Biography.*

APPENDIXES

A.

The following documents consist, with but one or two exceptions, of documentary materials hitherto unpublished. For the most part they are taken from the "Boswell Papers," *Additional Manuscripts 6394,* two volumes of letters and documents in the British Museum, London. The Boswell Papers contain letters and papers of Sir William Boswell, English Ambassador to the Dutch Netherlands from 1632 until the collapse of the government of Charles I during the English Civil Wars. Sir William was a Suffolk man, educated at Jesus College, Cambridge (Fellow, 1606; M.A., 1607). Until 1620, when he served as secretary to Lord Herbert of Cherbury, Ambassador to Paris, little is known of his activities.[1] Later, in 1622, he was secretary to John Williams, Bishop of Lincoln, and was employed also by George Abbot, Archbishop of Canterbury, to root out non-conformity in the eastern counties.[2] In 1624-25, Boswell was chosen Member of Parliament for Boston. During his parliamentary career he was appointed one of the "clerks extraordinary" to the Privy Council (1627-29), attended the Earl of Carlisle to Lorraine and Piedmont (1628) to stir up feeling against Richelieu after the failure of the expedition against LaRochelle, was named one of the "Keeper and Registers of the Papers and Records concerning matters of State and Council" (1629), and was occasionally associated with Sir Dudley Carleton in the latter's work as Ambassador to the Netherlands (1628-32).[3] In January, 1632, an English newswriter reported that Boswell was "designed by his Majesty to be resident in the Hague in

---

1 Godfrey Davies (ed.), *Autobiography of Thomas Raymond* [*Camden Society Publications,* Third Series, XXVIII (London, 1917)], Appendix II, 69-80; *Dictionary of National Biography.*

2 John Hackett, *Scrinia Reserata:* . . . (London, 1693), Part I, 86; see also two letters to Boswell, one unsigned, the other from the Archbishop of Canterbury in 1621-22, in *Boswell Papers,* I, fols. 25, 29-30.

3 *Calendar of State Papers, Domestic Series, James I, 1619-23,* 364, 379, 406, 465, 576; *ibid., 1623-25,* 171; *ibid., Charles I, 1627-28,* 131; *ibid., 1628-29,* 483, 531; *ibid., 1629-31,* 2, 182-83 ff.

place of Sir Dudley Carleton" and characterized him as "one of the ablest and honestest men of our nation."[4] Boswell was given his instructions July 11, 1632, sailed in August, and presented his credentials to the Dutch States General on September 7.[5] The next year (July 25, 1633) he was knighted by Lord Horatio Vere who held a commission for that purpose from Charles I, "the Resident [Boswell] making a large and eloquent oration in prayse of that most auncient and noble order of the Garter."[6]

Sir William was a zealous supporter of the Established Church and of the prerogative of the King. His activities in uprooting the Congregational classis and bringing to conformity English ministers to the Merchant Adventurers and chaplains of the English regiments in the Low Countries—for which Archbishop Laud gave him high praise[7]—are described herein. Later, when civil war started in England, Sir William assisted Queen Henrietta Maria to pawn the Crown Jewels in Holland.[8] Throughout the Civil Wars, Boswell was a valuable royalist agent in the Low Countries whose activities Strickland and other parliamentary agents strove to counteract. For his zeal against Parliament, Sir William's English properties were sequestered in 1643.[9] He died, broken-hearted and defeated, about 1649, soon after the execution of his beloved King.

Boswell's papers, particularly the first volume, contain important and hitherto little exploited sources relating to the English Congregationalists and other non-conformists in Holland between about 1620 and 1640. The second volume consists chiefly of letters between Sir William and Sir Simon D'Ewes, De Laet, and other learned men of the time. These letters, with others of a similar nature found with the correspondence of Constantine Huygens in the library of the Uni-

4 Davies, *Thomas Raymond*, 69.
5 *Calendar of State Papers, Dom. Ser., Chas. I, 1631-33*, 394, 412; *Archief van de Staten-Generaal*: "Registers van ordinaris resolutien" (1632), No. 581, fols. 430 b, 434. Carleton did not return to England until mid-November. See *ibid.*, fols. 522 b, 537, 537 b, 538, 539 b.
6 Davies, *Thomas Raymond*, 40; *Earl Cowper MSS, 12th Report of the Hist. MSS Comm.* (London, 1888), II, Appendix, Part II, 20.
7 Laud to Boswell, Lambeth, May 24, 1638, in *Boswell Papers*, I, fol. 298.
8 William Bray (ed.), *Diary of John Evelyn* (2nd ed., 2 vols., London, 1819), II, 39.
9 *Journal of the House of Commons*, III, 1642-44, 141.

versity of Leiden,[10] demonstrate that Boswell himself was no mean scholar of the theory of sound and that he was an early "experimental philosopher" such as later formed the "Invisible College" and the Royal Society of London. Considering their value and accessibility it is strange that the Boswell Papers have been employed so little by historians of Congregationalism and of Puritanism in general. As Champlin Burrage says, the papers have been "only casually used by Dr. John Waddington" and were "apparently unknown to Dr. Dexter."[11] Burrage made considerable use of Sir William's literary remains and he published parts of some of them;[12] but, except for a brief article by the present writer,[13] there appears to be no author who has attempted to present in connected fashion the story which is tortuously told in the Boswell Papers.

Besides documents drawn from the Boswell Papers, various letters and other manuscripts derive from the State Papers, Public Record Office, London, from other collections in the British Museum, and from one or two Dutch libraries. The attempt has been made to select materials that are especially significant to and illustrative of this study, and to reproduce no documents herein which are readily available in other published sources.

Some liberties are taken with the manuscripts. Anyone familiar with seventeenth century writings is aware of the now obsolete punctuation, spelling, and abbreviations then employed. In an effort to preserve the original "flavor" of the manuscripts, much of this old spelling has been retained; but abbreviations have been expanded where their meaning is not doubtful, and the punctuation has been modernized in the same fashion. Thus "℘," "m̄," "Matie," "or," "Bp," "wch," "ff," "wt," "ye," "yt," and the like are expanded to "per-," "pre-," or "pro-"; "mm"; 'Majestie"; "-or" or "our"; "Bishop"; "which"; "F-"; "what;" "the"; "that"; and so on, as are respectively required by modern forms. Some liberties are taken with capitalization as well. All words, letters, and phrases in square brackets are inserted by the editor.

10 See, for example, *Huygens 37*.
11 *The Early English Dissenters*, I, 281.
12 *Ibid.*, I, 304-305; II, 260 ff.
13 ''The New England Way in Holland,'' in *The New England Quarterly*, VI (December, 1933), 747-92.

I.

Copie Translated of Petition of some English Ministers
to his Majesty.   1621.   Concerning their Classis &c.[14]

Maye it please your moste Royall Majesty:
Wee your Majesties moste humble Subjects, ministers of the
Word of God residente in the Unyted provinces, Havinge
some three yeares paste felte your Majesties favour in your
kingly or Royall approbation of the presente remedy (at that
tyme propounded) for redresse of all enormities amongeste
[us], having also perceaved and felte the blessed and won-
derfull fruites followed thereuppon, in deportinge or putting
away of some scandalous parsons and entertayninge and putting in their places persons more fitt and of better worth
and in our uniformity and prosperous proceeding in all
Christian Consent with the churches where wee Live, and
the good contentment of our superiors under whome wee
exercyse our places; And now being againe assembled to
the same happy intents, and having had notice by your
Majestys Ambassador of your Majestys pleasure to sett
over us a Moderator to be appointed by your Majesty To have
an Insyghte uppon the direction of our affayres: Surceasing all
other proceedings wee have presently deliberated howe and in
what sorte wee were to carry and Comporte our selves in this
case That so we mighte be free from offence to God, Infidelity
to your Majesty and unthankfulnes to our presente Superiors;
And to our uttermoste apprehension, perceaving three things
to presente them selves: To wete, obedience or condescending
to your Majesties motion and will of nomination, or ells
surceauce of all Further Sinodale Proceedings, or, att Laste,
by information to your Majesty of the Inconveniences and
Impossibilities of these both, and the worthy fruite and profitt
of our presente course, Desyringe moste humbly your Majestys
favour in the continuation thereof, wee have held our selves to
this Laste, being (to our Judgmente) the sureste waye and
meanes to give satisfaction as well to God, to your Majesty,
as to the Estate wherein wee Live.

The firste beinge such That it hath no certainty of at-
tempte or beginninge nor Lykelyhood to obtayne it, because our

14 *Boswell Papers*, I, fols. 18-21.

firste and fondamentall Liberty or graunte to sett uppe or erecte
this ecclesiasticall freedom was expresly Limited unto us by the
deputies of the sinode of Southolland, Who desyred it, and by
acte of the Illustrious Lordes who graunted and consented it
onely uppon condition of our whole conformity with the churches of these provinces according to the example of the Wallon
churches, strangers as we are, which freedom wee also havinge
embraced and subscribed wee cannot, without breach of Infidel-
lity and wrong, revoke nor alter. As also by reason that the ministers of these churches (who much joyed in our uniformity
with them) were highly sorry when they heard of this comaund,
Bringing in such Innovations, Indurable miseries, and calamities
to this Estate, which, as they, but yet very Late, by too miserable
experiences which cannot yet be forgotten have found; So that
the ministers doe Judge it more fitt for the security and reste of
their churches, To lett us and our churches dissolve, rather
then that such a course, so strange unto them, should arryse
and take place amongeste them; which dissolution, howe easily
and suddenly they can Compasse and bringe to passe with the
Lordes Estates is wel knowne to such as desyre to know. That
all English and Skottish churches in these countries, excepte
twoo, doe wholy depende and have their being and entertayne-
mente of the favour and Love of the Lordes the States. And
the rather for that the feare of such a thing (as now appeareth)
hath detayned from us, with consent and supporte of certayne
provinces, some of our Reverente and beloved bretheren,
whose company (as we do much desyre and wishe for) wee
doe not doubte but to gett, that your Majesty wilbe pleased to
acquit or free us of this particular, for that the feare hath
bene so hurtfull as to take a disaffection or distaste of us,
what greate ill or hurte maye wee doubte for, that the expectation shall produce, beinge as is aforesaide.

The seconde: To wete, our Totall ruine and downefall is
such as cannot stande withoute apparante and unrevocable
stayne of our selves in pointe of unthankfulnes and neglect,
as well of your Majestys favor in approovinge as of the Lordes
Estates graunting unto us, our Liberties thus long enjoyed, or
of an Inexcusable Imputation of skandall to God in the neglect
of his churches in our Care, seing that certainly againe thereuppon will follow a spoyle of upryghte ordre and the confusions

which now in some sorte are trodden under feete come forth againe. And also this cannot be withoute forgetting, neglecting, or in contempte of your Majestys Subjects, as well ministers as others, within these provinces. The generalls, Coronells, and other officers honnoring our assemblyes, whose honnor and reputation begon to growe and to stand firme by this blessed bond of union, with the Comunion with them in these Christian ordonnances will now, by reason of our disunion, of necessity consume and come to nothinge.

The thirde which, to our Judgemente, onely can consiste, is in our oppinion free of all offence and fitt to give satisfaction to all menn, As wel for that menn doe know, that it is very acceptable to this State and very proffitable for their churches As for that it is the rather and the willinglyer embraced by our selves in respecte it is in no sorte offensive or hurtfull to the churches in your Majestys dominions, by reason of our publyke declaration and unrevocable protestation in accepting of it, of our Integrity towardes them, Confessinge in our soules and Consciences That wee doe holde them, and by Gods grace alwayes will holde and esteem them for the true churches of Chryste Equally as deere as our selves in his eyes, Resolving continually to communicate with them notwithstanding any difference of outwarde ordres; These dyvers meanes beinge by us attempted, withoute any disrespect, sensure, prejudice, separation, or Condemnation of the said churches, Reserving unto and for them all deer reverence and our continuall prayers, as well for them as our owne welfare; And having found that our small proofe and beginning in this cause Is seconded from heavenn with a Lucky and riche successe in these our few Sessions, so that the roote which already it hath takenn Cannot againe be rooted oute withoute perill of the spoyle of this vynyard which God hath here planted.

So it is that these causes, moste deere Soverayne, besydes a multitude of Inconveniences more (which are not to be hindered) To followe uppon the Leaste Innovation of our firme proceedings, wee doe in all humility shewe unto your Majestys eyes That which withoute doubte God Amighty hath putt into our harts; To wete, that it would please your Majesty of his speciall favor and grace To graunte and consente That wee maye goe forward and prosper in our former quyett and Com-

fortable proceedings as wee have begunn withoute any hinder
or Interruption; Having to this our moste humble requeste the
more hope and assurance when wee doe remember and recorde
your Majestye publyke oppinion concerning the uniformity,
power, and freedome of all princes and potentates in owtward
ordonances and disposition in Ecclesiasticall disciplyne in their
territoryes; And also because your Majesty is onely he, That
the world doe holde, to be the onely means and instrumente of
quenshing and Consuminge of Schismes and separations Lately kindled through the Vorstian and Arminian factions which
are Lyke more dangerously to ryse againe by reason of these
alterations amongeste us. The Dutch and French churches,
with whome wee converse to the Infamye and skandall of our
selfs and all our former actions, To expose and putt our selves
and our Congregations in the said perill of our Totall dissolution, whereby wee shalbe berefte and robbed of all comfortable
ordre and govermente, and of the Laudable meanes to make
knowne our Lawfull proceedings, As the Dutch and French
doe when they are requyred and as wee have donne as well
to the Lordes Estates generall, as to your Majesties Ambassador, which are the beste meanes whereby all ministers and
churches are keapte safe from faling into such faction and
schismes.

Wherefore moste mighty king, Wee your Majestys said
Subjects, doe caste ourselves uppon our knees for the person
of this our Brother Whome wee in all humility doe sende unto
your Majesty, prayinge that your favor and grace now againe
and ever maye shyne uppon us to the renewinge of our happy
hopes, refreshinge of all sorrowfull hartes, and comforte of
all those with whome wee converse. The which, together with
us, will thanke God almighty for your Majesties experimented
former favors and for these that at this presente are moste
humbly desyred. And shall Jointly pray &c.

II.

Declaration or Act of the English Classis for preventing
of Jealousies &c.: of the English Church &c.: About A.
Dei: 1620.[15]
The said Ministers for the removall of all jealousies of

15 *Boswell Papers*, I, fol. 17. Copy.

innovation, Separation, faction or schisme did all jointly and severally protest that as they did intertaine the benefites and libertie of the said order and governement to be practised and adminestered only according to the French Churches, and as is contained in the graunt from the Most Illustrious Lords the States, without any purpose or intention to doe any thing in any other forme to the least offence of the churches in these Provinces, or any way to impaire any particular lawfull privelege, which hitherto hath bene enjoyed by any of the Inglisch churches in These provinces, being in nature or quality naither offensive nor contrary to the order of the Dutch or French Churches among whome they reside, nor any way repugnant to the power and graunt foresaid: so likewise did they also protest their intertainment of the said order and forme to be (notwithstanding the bond of our Uniforme obedience to the power and graunt foresaid during their abode in those parts) free in their souls and consciences from any disrespect, censure, prejudice or condemnation of the churches in His Majestys dominions, reserving unto them all due reverence and acknowledgment, as to the true churches of Christ, equally precious in the sight of God (through the same most precious faith) with our selves; resolving still to hold communion with them notwithstanding any difference of externall order; and evermore to pray for and procure their happines and welfare with their owne—

> Jhon Forbes [Delft]
> Jhon Wing [The Hague]
> Thomas Scott [Utrecht]
> Thomas Barkelay [Rotterdam]
> Walter Whetstone ["preacher to the Regiment of Viscount Lisle"]
> Andrew Hunter [Scots army chaplain]
> Jhon Hassall [The Hague]
> George Clarke
> Samuell Bachiler ["preacher to the Regiment of Sir Charles Morgan Knight and Colonel"]
> Alexander Clarke
> Jhon Oswald.

III.

Copie translated of the Letter of some English Ministers
to the States General for an English Classis, &c. 1621.[16]
To the High and Mighty Lordes
My Lordes the States Generall of the Unyted Provinces, &c.
High and mighty Lordes,

Wee the Ministers and preachers of Gods Worde of the
English and Scottish nation, Being assembled att Rotterdam,
by vertue and order of your highnesses special favor graunted
unto us at the requeste of the Sinode of Southolland, with
approbation of his Majesty our kinge (as wee understood by
his Majestys Ambassador) for to proceede to the reformation
of such disordres and confusions as menn did too well and
openly perceave in dyvers of the English and Skotch ministers
as they sayde or pretended to be, in these quarters or provinces,
There was from the said Lord Embassador shewen unto us a
Letter thereby requyring of us to sende unto him some or any
of our Congregation to understand his Majestys pleasure before to proceede any further in our Sinodale affaires which
being so-donne, and our deputy returninge, and telling us on
behalfe of the said Lord Ambassador That it was his Majestys
pleasure that wee should nominate twoo or three of our beste
qualifyed persons Owte of the which his Majesty mighte
choose one to moderate our assembly, and to have an Insighte
on all our proceedings. And that, until that were donne and
his Majestys pleasure were heard thereuppon, men shoulde
proceede no further in the Sinode, whereuppon wee seriously
takinge in our Considerations howe wee mighte beste Comporte, behave, or acquyte ourselves, withoute offence to God
and his truth, Infidelity to our king and unthankfulnes to your
highnesses, whose favor wee feele and under whose protection
wee breathe, Live, and enjoye these priviledges both parsonall
and nationall, In which deliberation to our beste understanding wee coulde bethinke no better waye in this cause, To
wete, for with the Consente, favor, and advyce of your Lordshipps To sende oute from us a parson To informe our kinge
as well of your hyghnesses favor as of his Royall consente
thereunto, and of the blessings and benefitt The churches here
in generall and wee our selves in particular already have felte

16 *Boswell Papers,* I, fols. 22-23.

and lykely are yet to follow by the continuation thereof. Humbly beseeching That your highnesses wilbe pleased to approve and allowe of this our resolution, whereof your Lordshipps by this annexed coppye shall the better understand our meaninge which wee are mynded and doe intende to presente unto his Majesty. And accordingly for the advauncemente of the same to graunte unto us, your highnesses favorable Letters of recomendation, &c.

IV.

English Preachers in the Netherlands.[17]

Of the Regiments

Lord Vere. Mr. [Stephen] Goffe.
Gen. Morgan.   Mr. [Samuel] Batchelor.
Col. Paginham.   Mr. Day.
Col. Herbert.   Mr. Sclaer.

Of the Merchants

Mr. [John] Forbes and his assistant
Mr. [Thomas] Hooker.

Garrisons

Utrecht.   Mr. [Isaac] Fortree.
Gorinchem. Mr. Batchelour. idem.
Tergoo. Mr. Day. idem.
Gittrodenberge. Mr. Firsby.
Busch [Bois-le-Duc].   Mr. Gribbins
Husden.   Mr. Widdows.
Bergen.   Mr. Paine.
Dort. a Dutchman which speakes English.
Nimmegen.   Mr. Sibbald. Scotchman.
Wesell. A Dutchman which speakes English.
Tiel. Mr. Sclaer. idem.
Doesborough. Mr. Parsons.

Townes

Amsterdam. Mr. [John] Pagett.
Rotterdam. Mr. [Hugh] Peters.
Flushing. Mr. [John] Roe.
Middleborough. Mr. Drake.
Leyden. Mr. [Hugh] Goodyer.
Hage. Mr. [Samuel] Balmford.

The towne Ministers have meanes allowed them by the States. Of the Garrisons none have any Meanes from the

17 *Boswell Papers*, I, fol. 175. Published also in Burrage, *Early English Dissenters*, II, 276-78.

States but only Utrecht. 500 g. per ann. and Bergen 200 g. per ann.; the rest are payed by the Captaines, which is about 2 gulders a weeke, as long as they bee in the Garrisons. So that when they are in the fielde they have nothing but only of those Companies which are left at home.

Of all those there belong to the English classis Mr. Forbes, Mr. Peters, Mr. Balmsford, Mr. Batchelour, Mr. Paine, Mr. Widdowes, Mr. Sibbald. This last came within this yeare (and though they have had noe classicall meeting) yet must be named here because hee was declared by the authority of the classis at Nimmegen, and doth reckon himselfe of that classis.

Those that refuse to be of the English Classis, some are of the Dutch and some are of none. Mr. Pagett, Mr. Fortree, Mr. Gribbins are of the Dutch. (What Mr. Roe and Mr. Drake doe is not knowne, but they refuse to be of the English Classis). Mr. Goodyere desired to be of the Leyden Classis, but they will not admitt him. And the reason is because they doe observe by a longe and Sharpe controversy which hath been betwixt him & his parishioners, He is of a rigider Discipline then of the Dutch Discipline is [sic].

Mr. Gribbins was commended by the Lord Vere to the Busch, being a Palatinate man that wanted meanes, & having studied well in England. The officers report nothing but well of him.

Mr. Fortree was chosen by the officers, and is well approved of by them for a quiet man.

Mr. Paine was called from Schonehoven by the Englishe Classis to Bergen op Zome; after that by their Authority they had deprived one Mr. Clarke the Scotch regiment Preacher to the Earle of Bucklough.

Mr. Parsons is the regiment preacher to Coll: Belford. (it is likely hee is of no Classis at all.) Mr. Sibbald: to Coll: Broze.

V.

A true Relation of the first Erection of an English Church in Utrecht. With the proceedinge since.[18]

Before the yeare 1622 there was noe settled Congregation but only Regiment Preachers who during the tyme that the

---

18 *Boswell Papers*, I, fols. 270-75. Parts of this manuscript have been published in Burrage, *Early English Dissenters*, II, 286-90.

soldiers were in Garrison preached unto them; but they goeinge into the field the English Citizens and inhabitants were destitute of preachinge and other divine administrations.

Upon which occasion some of the most eminent of the Cittizens of the English nation propounded among them to erect a settled Congregation, because they were of a good number; which they could not doe without permission of the Lords the Staites of the Province, and Magistrates of the City of Utrecht. The Chiefe difficultie beinge then to finde meanes for the maintenance of the Minister.

Wherupon they made a muster of the families & inhabitants and found them to be about 120 in number, whoe framed a petition, which they all signed with their owne hands, and sent one Ralph Wase and Ephraim Buttler into the Haghe unto Sir Dudley Carelton, then Lord Ambassadour of his Majestie of Great Britaine, entreating his Letters of recomendation to the Lords the Staites of this Province that they would be pleased to graunt them some meanes for the Minister and permitt them to erect a Congregation &c. Which the said Lord Ambassador upon their request did, which petition of the Cittizens and Letter of the Lord Ambassador are yet to be seene in the Staites Chamber dated 20th April 1622.

The said Cittizens of the English Nation in Utrecht petitioned the Staite of the Province and Magistrates of the Citty of Utrecht for a grant of a church to meet in, and for a stipend towards the maintenance of their Minister.

The States Consented and allowed 150 gulders yeerly towards the Preachers maintenance, and thee Citty allowed as much, and the Church of St. Katherine was designed them for their meetinge in common with the soldiers of the Brittish nation; which was done the 8th of May, 1622, as we finde it recorded by Mr. Thomas Scott his owne hand, the first Minister of this settled Congregation.

The said Thomas Scott hath likewise recorded that then the Captains joyned with the Cittizens and, desirous to have an English Preacher, sent expresse messengers to Mr. Thomas Scott, then Preacher of the English Garrison at Gorchum, to call him to this place, and they promised (to witt, the Cittizens) to make a certaine stipend of 600 gulders by the yeare, and to allow him a house, and that besides he should have the benefitt of the Garrison, which was 2g by the short moneth of every syngle Companie and rateably of the rest.

The Consent of the states of this Province, dated the 14 May, and of the Citty, dated the 13th May, 1622, is with a proviso, that they (to witt, the congregation) shall not goe to thee Callinge of a minister then with[out] dew Correspondence, and examination of the Minister to which purpose they of the Citty gave Commission unto the Schepen Wittenwell and Vander Lynghen of the Citty Counsell.

The aforenamed Mr. Scott, beinge called, he was inducted by Mr. John Forbes, Preacher to the Marchants Adventurers at Delft, whoe then preached, Mr. Barckley, preacher at Rotterdam, Mr. Andrew Hunter, preacher to the Scottish Regiment, and Mr. Gualter Whitestone, preacher to the Regiment of Viscount Lisle. Also there were present the Committyes of the States and Magistrates, besides divers English officers of the Garrison then at Utrecht, with all dew solemntie on the 20th May, 1622.

The Cittizens of the English and Scottish nation resident at Utrecht made amongst them a muster of them that were able for to furnish the 300 g which they had promised to make the 600 g, and every one of the Contributors names, and to their promised contribution, set down in a List, and performed it accordingly, as divers of them that are yet alive and then were contributors can testifie.

The contribution continued but one year, and because there were many to whom this contribution fell heavy, the Congregation resolved againe to entreate the aforenamed Lord Embassadour to write in their hehalfe for increase of meanes, which he did accordingly and used divers reasons, that they were Cittizens, & ought not to be treated otherwise then the other Cittizens, and also as the French nation, and other more reasons, as by the said Letter in the States Chamber of this Province is yet to be seene.

Havinge obtained this Letter, Mr. Thomas Scott writes with his own hand in the records of the Church that the 12th of June in place of change of Church officers the Elders were continued because the Ministers stipend being not yet fully settled it was thought fitt to employ them still in the businesse, who were best acquainted with it. And also because the Church.

7

being newly gathered, the Deacons were best acquainted with such members as had need of assistance, and with the estate of those that should assist and contribute. Then they put up a request unto the States and another to the Magistrates of the Citty for increase of meanes towards the maintenance of the Minister, that soe the Cittizens of the English nation might be eased. The states granted an increase of 100 *g* yearly and the Magistrates the like summe, so that the Minister from the States and Magistrates received yearly 500 *g*. and from the citizens 100 *g* and this was paid quarterly by equall portions.

In June, 1625, the Preacher, Elders, and Deacons of the English Congregation petitioned to the States and Magistrates of the Citty that because the Church of St. Katherine was somewhat soe farr out of the way, that they might have againe the use of St. Peters Church; And procured to that end the Letters of recommendation of Henry, Earle of Oxford, and Generall Cicill, which was granted unto them, and tooke new possession thereof 24th July, 1625.

The 8th of June, 1626, Mr. Thomas Scott was killed goeing to the Church by one John Lambert, Soldier of Viscount Wimbleton Company.

The Consistorie of the English Congregation, fearing that their church might fall to the ground, being but newly raised, writ the 19th of June Letters in the name of the Congregation to one Mr. Jeremie Elbrough then at Montford, Lamenting their heavy losse, entreated his presence to accompanie the dead corps, and to conferre with him further in accepting the place of Mr. Scott.

The Said Mr. Elbrough came, yet could not accept the call Untill he was freed from Colonel Levistone, to whose regiment he was lately taken to be minister, which leave he shortly after obtained.

The 20th June the Synod of the English and Scotch Nation was kept at Utrecht, and the Elders put up a petition to the said Utrecht, and the Elders put up a petition to the said synod that the said Elbrough might be admitted for their pastor, which was granted, whereupon the synod with the Elders put up requests to the Lords the States and Magistrates of the City that they would be pleased to afford Mr. Elbrough the same allowance to be continued to him as was before granted to

Mr. Scott; which requests were granted, and the same meanes continued.

Then the Elders and Deacons acquainted their Pastor, Mr. Elbrough, how many of the Cittizens were not able to pay the summe that was formerly agreed on generally to make up the yearly 200 *g*, vid:t 100 *g* to the Preacher, the other to the Reader: Whereupon Mr. Elbrough discharged them of his stipend, and left it free to some of abilitie to give which were before bound by covenant to pay.

Mr. Jeremy Elbrough, having received Letters testimonial out of England as he was injoyned by the Synod, was confirmed in his pastoral charge of the English Church at Utrecht by Mr. John Forbes, Preacher to the English Merchants at Delft, on Thursday the 11th of June, 1627. There were present Mr. Samuell Batcheler, Preacher to the Regiment of Sir Charles Morgan, Knight and Colonel: Mr. Flaman, one of the Dutch Preachers of the Citty; also John Tunis Utenwall, one of the Magistrates of the Citty, with Captaines English of the Garrison, and the Burgers of the City.

The 29th August, 1627, upon the request of the Minister, Elders, and Deacons of the Church, the states and Magistrates of the Citty allowed eich an augmentation of 50 *g* by the year: soe that now the States and the Magistrates eich of them have given and doe give still 300 *g* yearly.

Note that all this while the English Church at Utrecht was governed by it selfe, and many disputes and questions thereof arising troubled as well the states as Magistrates, and the Classis they tooke notice thereof, and resolved to make them member of the Classis, yet did they continue by themselves as long as Mr. Elbrough was here.

In the year 1629 Mr. Elbrough was called to be Minister at Hambrough to the English Merchants there, and in his place succeeded Doctor Alexander Leighton, a Scottchman, and at his beinge taken on there was observed the Order of the Classis, as alsoe he tooke session with them and the English was admitted as a Member of the Classis.

But for some disputes about not preachinge on holly days as are here observed, he left the place, whom succeeded in the same year, 1629, one Mr. Ralph Clayton and both these men but a short tyme here.

The 29th of Sept., 1630, Mr. Isaac Fortrye, upon the departure of Mr. Ralph Clayton, was ordayned Pastor of the said English Church by Mr. Hugh Goodyeere, Minister of the English Church at Leyden, being recommended by the right worthy Sir Ferdinando Knightley, knight, serjeant-major to the Regiment of Colonell Herbert. And the said Mr. Fortrye hath taken alsoe the meanes which the officers and soldiers of the English Garrison had given formerly to his Predecessors.

But Mr. Fortrye having some private businesse of his owne was desirous to retire him home into England, and to leave this church, whereupon on the 29th June, 1637, he desired of the Consistorie his demission, and alsoe assistance to procure the like of the States and Magistrates for him: which the Consistorie [did] for as much as lay in them Condiscended unto; but on condition that he should not leave them untill he had procured them an able and Learned man to succeed him capable of the place.

Whereupon the Consistory (called the 4th of July, 1637) all them that formerlie had borne office in the Church to have their advise for the calling of another Minister, because they had already obtayned from the states and Magistrates leave to dismisse Mr. Fortrye and to looke out for another minister. The Apostiles or grants of the States and Magistrates contayninge both a restraynt not to proceed otherwise then according to the orders of the church of the Province and the old ordinary Custome, and that he that shall be called shall without any Contradiction conforme him to the Churches orders of this province.

Upon which permission or grant the Consistorie, old and new, tooke into consideration if before their callinge of another Minister they ought not to acquaint the officers English gone out of Garrison. Whereupon it was held meet that all good Correspondence should be held with them, but that as yet it was not tyme until they had pitcht upon a man, and called him, and that then they should be acquainted with it. And proceedinge to nomination by a generall voyce Mr. Samuel Wardd, Minister at Ipswich in England, was pitched upon, and resolved to acquaint the Lords the states and Magistrates with the nomination, entreatinge leave for to proceed to an effectuall call.

Accordingly, they acquainted both states and Magistrates whoe did like well of the man and gave them leave to proceed to the effectual calling with this reservation to observe in all proceedings the orders of the Church of this Province, Accordinge to which permission the Consistorie passed an act of the call, and Mr. Isaac Fortrye was to goe into England to present it.

Before his departure the said Mr. Isaac Fortrye spake with Sir Ferdinando Knightley (then by accident in this towne) acquaintinge him with the business and proceedinge whoe did like well of it, and undertook to acquaint the officers then at the siege of Breda with it.

Mr. Fortrye returned out of England the first of September, 1637, and the 3d of September Assembled the Consistorie old and new, and related unto them the successe of his Voyadge, that Mr. Wardd had excused the call, as by a letter from Mr. Wardd unto the Consistorie he made it appeare.

The 14th of September, 1637, the Consistorie old and new were upon this and an other occasion againe assembled and was by Mr. Fortrye againe desired to be dismissed, and that the Consistorie would looke out for another man; and because they were mett in amplissima forma, they proceeded to the nominatinge of a man and far most voyces fell on Mr. Amarant, yet was the Effectuall call deferred untill it should be asked him, that if he should be called, he would fully submitt him to the Church orders established by the synod by which by the Apostilles on our requests we are bound unto, and that he should procure some Testimonie of his life and doctrine; which questions being asked him, he answered yea, and to the other promised to doe.

In the meantyme Mr. Paule Amarant went to the Leager before Breda with Letters from Mr. Fortrye and from Mr. Skinner in the name of the Consistorie to Sir Ferdinando Knightley, Knight &c., acquaintinge him with the proceedings.

Mr. Fortrye had in the meanwhile procured a demission of the deputies of the Classis of Utrecht, without which he could not with credit depart this place, as having bene a member of the same Classis all the tyme of his abode in this Citty; and he went away the 9th of October, 1637.

The place now beinge Vacant, the Consistorie presented to the states and Magistrates requests acquaintinge them with the nomination and desired for the effectuall call, which was by both granted as can appeare by the Appostilles dated the 11th and 16th October, 1637, all with the proviso to observe the Order of the Church of this Province.

The Leave beinge obtayned, the Consistorie acquainted the Dutch minister some inqualitie as our next neighbours and others as deputies of the Classis.

Whereupon they came into the Consistorie the 19th October, 1637, and, as deputies of the Classis, beinge made acquainted with our proceedings, desired their Assistance accordinge to Order (because we were destitute of a Minister) to proceed to the effectuall call.

They demanded if we were assured of all necessarie qualities of the man, and for Testimonialls for his gifts the Consistorie was contented for his learninge they themselves could judge, and Testimonialls be produced from three several Ministers which were approved and allowed of; And further all things beinge considered, he was received to be our ordinarie Pastor, to which end we passed an Act in forma, accordinge to the synodicall order.

This solemnitie of the callinge beinge passed, the Consistorie resolved to proceed to the Establishinge, and therefore published this call on 3 severall Sundayes following, on Sunday the 22nd October, 1637, the first; the 29th Octob. the second; and the 5th of November the third publication, to the end that if there were any that had any thinge to speake or alledge against the said Paul Amerant his life or doctrine they might speake in tyme and place conveynient.

The 4th of November in the evening some of the English officers of the Garrison of Utrecht sent for Steven Taylor and Sent him to John Bor and Thomas Skynner, elders, to require them to surcease the third publication(which was to be done the next morninge) untill Mr. Amerant had brought testimonie out of England from Gentry and Cleargie, which the said Bor and Skynner could not condiscend unto as not beinge Consistorially mett, yet sent backe to the officers that they saw noe cause why the third publication should be surceased, because their was noe evidence brought in against the man &c.   Yet that they thought it would be reasonable for not to disgrace the man to let the publication goe on, and that before the confirmation they would be willinge to heare them and enter into communication with them.   The next morninge before sermon the said Elders assembled the Consistorie, old and new, to acquaint them what was happened and asked their advise; and was by farre the most voyces concluded that the publication should goe on, which was done accordingely.

The 7th November, 1637, the Classis was kept at Utrecht upon which the English Church hath ordinarily her Minister and an Elder where by the deputies of the Classis and the Elder of the Church was related what was passed, whoe approved and liked well of the Proceedinges, and Ordered that the confirmation should be done the next Lords day followinge.

Yet because the Consistorie had proffered to the officers that before the confirmation they would be willinge to enter into Communication, and from them noe body appearinge, Mr. John Bor, one of the Elders, went to divers of the officers, and Mr. Amerant to them all, acquaintinge them with the resolution of proceedinge the next day followinge.

The 12th November, 1637, Mr. Amerant was inducted and established in the English Church at Utrecht by Mr. Brigidius Van Viana, Minister at Jutphaes, with dew solemnitie. And there were present, besides divers Captaines and gentlemen of the English Nation, divers Dutch men of qualitie, with the Heere Van Renswow, one of the Provinciall states, the chief Burgemaster of the Cittie, Vander Holick,[19] Doctor Voetius, Divinity Professor of the Academy in Utrecht, and Mr. Flaman, one of the Dutch Preachers in the said Citty. Which came all off their own accord, as often frequenting the English Church, besides divers Dutch gentlemen and Canonicks that are members of the Congregation.

VI.

Articles exhibited & delivered unto the Synod of the English & Scottish Ministers in the Netherlands, in the name of his Majestie of Great Brittanie, by the right honorable the Lord Carleton, Baron of Ambercourt, Ambassador extraordinarie to the States Generall of the Unit-

19 "Secritary Hilton" had been inserted after Vander Holick and crossed out.

ed Provinces, May 19, 1628. [With the ministers' reply, dated at Rotterdam, June 4, 1628.][20]

1.   It is his Majesties pleasure, that the said Ministers meddle not with the making or composing, much lesse the publishing of any new Liturgie or sett forme of prayer for their congregations.

2.   That they by no meanes do exercise the power of Ordination; but that they leave both English & Scottish to receive holy orders only from their owne mother-churches established in those two kingdomes; and that they accept of no other into any pastorall charge, but those only who have beene so ordained.

3.   That they bring in no novelties in any rites or Ceremonies which either concerne the actuall admission of Lawfull ministers unto their pastorall charge, or which may be used in any other sacred act whatsoever.

4.   That they assume no power to themselves to meddle with any point of doctrine; but that in doctrinall points they keepe themselves to what hath beene established by the English & Dutch Churches.

5.   His Majestie is well content that they should still keepe that power, which King James his Royall Father intended to them; viz: To suppresse those who tooke upon them the function of preachers without lawfull vocation or Admission to the Ministery.   And 2ly. to examine, restraine, & punish the ill manners of such as give scandall by their vitious lives.   And moreover his Majestie doth recommend unto them, to make diligent inquisition after those who write books or pamphletts any way derogatory to the Church or state of England; & as much as in them lieth to suppresse them.

6.   In case any doubt or difficulty arise concerning the true meaning or execution of these particulars; that they then repaire to his Majesties Ambassador or Agent for the time being, who will ever have, or be able to procure, such directions from his Majesty whereby so godly a worke may be duely & rightly advanced.

Signed,
D. Carleton.

20 *Boswell Papers*, I, fols. 40-44.   Copy.   Portions of this document are published in Burrage, *Early English Dissenters*, II, 264-70.

[The ministers' reply, Rotterdam, June 4, 1628.]

May it please your Sacred Majestie graciously to receive
& Consider this humble declaration of us your Majesties most
loyall & dutifull subjects (the English & Scotch Ministers)
now living under the power of a forraine state, touching these
articles exhibited unto us in your Majestys name as your Royall
pleasure, by the right honorable the Lord Carleton, Baron of
Imbercourt, your Majestys Ambassador extraordinary to the
States Generall of the United Provinces the 29th of May, 1628.

First in generall, we humbly beseech your Royall Majestie
to consider how unjustly without any occasion by us, ministers
to these churches of England & Scotland, a needles trouble
hath beene raised unto us, First in the time of King James
of happy memory & now againe in your Majesties time upon
some sinister suggestions only, as though our proceedings in
our Synodall assemblies should be derogatory to the Churches
of the said kingdomes; whereas that solemne protestation made
by us to the contrary att our first embracing & undertaking
that authority given us by the most Illustrious Lords the States
Generall by the procurement of his Majesties Ambassador doth
sufficiently cleare us of that imputation; the contents of which
protestation here following we humbly present to your Majestie.[21]

.   .   .   .

Secondly, we humbly beseech your Majestie to take notice
of the most wise, religious, & just resolution of your Majesties
father of happy memory, not only practised but also published
by him, not to meddle with any but those within the precincts
of his owne dominions, & to leave it absolutely free to every
Christian King, Prince, & Commonweale to prescribe unto
theirs the enternall forme of Ecclesiasticall governement, which
godly pattern, if it shall please your Majestie to follow on our
behalfe, (who although by birth we acknowledge our selves
your Majesties subjects, yett by our present state & being are
subject to the authority of the most Illustrious Lords the States
Generall) your Majestie shall not only manifest your owne
piety & justice to the world, but also shall free us, your
Majesties humble subjects, from much trouble; & particularly

21 The "protestation" which follows is precisely the same, without signatures
    added, as that printed in Appendix II above.

from that perplexity betweene two dangerous extremes whereinto we are cast by being subject in one & the selfe same thing
to two severall, distinct, & supreme authorities; whereby it must
of necessity follow, that some time now or then we must
inevitably draw the displeasure of the one or other upon us; it
being impossible for us to serve two Masters offending neither.

Besides this general consideration, we humbly beseech
your Majestie to accept of these our answers to the particular
articles.

Ans. 1.   Concerning the making or publishing of any new
Liturgie.   We are sorry that our best intentions are so mis-
construed, it never havinge entred into our minds to frame or
publish any new Liturgie or to oppose or condemne the Liturgies
of any other Churches; but only to enlarge that allready extant
which by authority & command of the States we are enjoyned
to observe by adding there unto from other Liturgies; & among
the rest from the Liturgie of England so much as without
offense or scandall in these Churches might be practised; which
foresaid Liturgie hath beene in continuall use in all Churches
here from the time of Queen Elizabeth of famous memory,
Whilst the Earle of Leicester did governe in these provinces;
& agreed upon & practised in the Churches of the Brill &
Vlissinghe, then absolutly depending upon the authority of the
Kings of England & maintained by them.   Such was the care
of your Majestys royall predecessors to have all things among
their subjects here residing to be done in conformity to the
Churches of these lands, thereby to prevent all offense, & to
maintaine the peace & unitie of the Church: which course we
trust assuredly, your Majestie intends we should follow; not
purposing we should putt in practise any Liturgy never as yett
authorized in these parts; or that we should leave every man
to his owne liberty to use what Liturgie he pleaseth: seing
thereby as great, if not greater confusion & disorder should
raigne amongst us after order established, as was before the
erection of our Synode.

Touching the practise of Ordination forbidden us in the
2d article: We humbly beseech your Majestie to weigh the
nature of ordination, being an essential point of the function
of our Ministery for the well ordering the house of God over
which we are sett, as well as the preaching of the gospell &

administration of the Sacraments; so that with good conscience we cannot omitt it, nor leave it wholly to others without being guilty of neglect of the office laid upon us by Christ. And we are persuaded, that your Majestie, considering this, will never prohibitt us the exercise of anything the power whereof is conferd upon us by Him, there being (as we hope) no just cause in our persons or carriadge to the contrary.

2. Ordination is of such a nature that the exercise thereof being taken from us, the practise of all other points of Ecclesiasticall discipline over others of the Ministery are taken away with it: Seing none can displace that have no power to place, nor take away authority where they cannot give it. The Ordainors may maintaine the ordained by them against all others; it being the order of all Churches that Ministers in their Ministery be subject to their Ordainors. This point is also confirmed by the Popes owne law Caus. 9, quaest. 2. where is said, Qui ordinare non poterit, quomodo judicabit? nulla tenus procul dubio judicabit, aut judicare poterit.

3. If we should leave this practise wholly to these Churches, & thereby leave to them all the rest of the points of Ecclesiasticall governement, we consequently give way to a forraine Ecclesiasticall power over the Churches within the dominions of this State; & so should not only prove ourselves most unthankfull persons, but also wrong the state, in transferring the liberty & power graunted us by them to strangers, so enthralling them to a forraine authority.

4. Your Majestie may consider what infamy & disgrace by this course shall be brought upon us, your Majestys subjects, as the only men in these Churches who are unworthy to enjoy the freedome which other strangers (& namely the French) do peaceably possesse. We beseech your Majestie graciously to respect the credit of your owne loyall subjects, that they be not herein made inferior in estimation to other strangers, & so exposed to the prophane derision & contempt of all men.

5. We beseech your Majestie to ponder what a dangerous precedent this were to have the practise of any affaires Ecclesiasticall to depend upon a forrain power without the limits of the kingdome or state where it is exercised. What confusion should fall amongst States & Princes, if once this practise should take place? For why may not a forrain civill power

order the affaires of another state, if a forraine Ecclesiasticall
power shall once have place to order the Ecclesiasticall affaires
of another State? Was not this a speciall reason which moved
your Majestys Father of happy memory to take such paines in
writing that famous apologie pro juramento fidelitatis against
such usurped power by the Pope? We beseech your Majestie
to consider if any state under heaven, except papisticall, would
willingly suffer such a practise so dangerous to creepe in & take
place in their dominions; considering that even in this point of
ordaining of Ministers, the Popes owne law doth not permitt
a Bishop to ordaine any without the limits of his owne Bishoprick, much lesse in a forrain state, as hereby doth manifestly
appeare Caus. 9. quaest. 2. Nullus primas, nullus Metropolitanus,
Nullus reliquorum Episcoporum alterius adeat civitatem, aut
ad possessionem accedat, quae ad cum non pertinet. Item
Episcopum non debere alienam irruere Civitatem, quae illi
probatur non esse subjecta; Neque in regionem quae ad ejus
curam minime noscitur pertinere. Item, nullum Episcopum
audere debere ex aliam provinciam ad aliam transitum facere,
& ordinare aliquos in Ecclesia, aut preferre ad sacrum Min-
isterium. Item, Episcopi qui extra suam Diocesin sunt, ad
Ecclesias quae extra terminos carum sunt, non accedant, neque
confundant aut permisceant Ecclesias, secundum regulas
statutas. Item, Non invitati Episcopi ultra Diocesin accedere
non debent super ordinandis aliquibus, vel quibuscunque dis-
ponendis Ecclesiasticis causis, servatar regular, suprascriptar
Manifestum namque est, quod per singulas quasque provincias
provincialis Synodus administrare & gubernare omnia debeat.
6. We beseech your Majestie to conceive that if we should continue a Synodall body without practise of ordination, we should
be such an Ecclesiasticall body as is not to be found in any
reformed Church in the world. And therefore we leave it
unto your Majestys wise judgement, if the leaving this practise
wholly to the Churches of England and Scotland should not
worke in all abroad a greater distaste of the Churches of
England & Scotland, & Episcopall governement in them (if
once it begin to extend its authority to forraine nations without the compasse of your Majesties dominions) for suppressing
in their owne brethren abroad the ordinary practise of all
other reformed Churches? May not all Churches thinke, yea

do they not allready conceive hereby, that if they could they would both condemne & overthrow all their governement? Whereas otherwise, they might have all other Churches to hold peace & communion with them, if they should not incroach so strangely upon them & their practise in our persons.

7. We beeseech your Majestie to consider whether the Churches of England & Scotland will take upon them to ordaine Pastors for Churches in forraine parts wherein they have no authoritie, & wherein the Churches can have no dependence on them, as being under another State whereof they are not members? We persuade ourselves that they will not; & that for divers reasons:

1. Because we judge, they will avoid in their persons that vice so-much condemned in the Scriptures, which is Πολυπραγμονεῖν, ἀλλοτριοεπισκοπεῖν [ἀλλότρια ἐπισκοπεῖν?] καὶ περιεργάζεσθαι. Seing even the Popish canons do condemne this, as is shewed.

2. Because we thinke they will not practise themselves that which they & all reformed Churches condemne in the Bishop of Rome: in whom amongst other things, this is not esteemed the least part of the marke of his Anti-Christianisme, That he will have all other Churches subject to him. All usurpation of authority over other Churches in a forrain state being meerely papall, as doth manifestly appeare Caus. 9. quaest. 3. nunc vero where it is said Licet apostolicâ prerogativâ possum de qualibet Ecclesia [?] clericum ordinare. Item. per principalem, where is also said, Potestalem & jus habemus, nonsolum in Monachos verum etiam in quoslibet clericos de quacunque dioecesi.

Lastly, we beeseech your Majestie to consider That all-though they would take this upon them, whether the Churches of this land will admitt among them any such practise, not only for the respects above declared, but also for the hurt and danger which this difference betwixt them & us might breed unto their State allready too much shaken & weakned by intestine questions & oppositions among themselves of this kinde; whereby their union & communion is allready not a little rent. As also if we should upon this occasion cause any alienation betwixt them (as undoubtedly by this practise we should, seeing the feare of it allready makes them not only neglect us, but also to oppose the standing of our Synodall authority). What can we expect but the utter deprivation of all the benefitt of our freedome in matters of religion, or the forcing us to be no Churches att all; or else to become subject members unto them which they have, & do attempt. We leave it therefore to your Majestys wise consideration whether it stands not more for your Majestys honor, the good & content of the churches of England & Scotland, & the credit of us, your Majestys poore subjects, that we subsist a free & entire body of our selves, then to be swallowed up by incorporation with strangers. Touching the last clause of the 2d art. not to receive any other unto Pastorall charge, but those only who have beene so ordained:

1. Your Majestie may please to take knowledge from us That we neither have nor do call that ordination into question; but do & still intend to receive such as are so ordained except there be other just reason to the contrary.

2. We beseech your Majestie to consider what wrong we should do to all other reformed Churches, & particularly to the Churches of this state wherein we live, if we should so slight them as to reject in the midst of themselves (we being but strangers) such as have beene or shall be ordained by them. What were this else, but to call into question the lawfullnes & sufficiency of ordination in other reformed Churches & to approve of none but of that which comes from the Churches of England & Scotland only? There can be nothing injoyned whereby to make us more odious & distastfull to all Churches reformed besides then this: it arguing plainly a professed separation from them. As for the inconveniency that might be feared to follow upon our liberty of ordination, your Majesty may rest assured that it cannot follow by our practise, because we neither have nor do intend ever to ordaine any but such as shall have actuall employment among ourselves in a particular charge. So as they cannot leave their charge unlesse they be orderly dismissed. But if this liberty of ordination be taken from us, it will, & must needs, fall into the hands of the Dutch preachers; & so that inconveniency which is feared from us may probably arise in greater measure from them. Touching the 3d. Art. We are sorry, that either ignorantly or maliciously our lawfull orderly proceedings in conformity to all reformed churches, both in admission of

Ministers into their places & in other sacred acts, have beene so traduced to your Majestie with the name of novelties & other disgracefull termes; since we have practised nothing but that which we are able to justifie to be both commendable, comely, & conforme to ancient & present practise of other Churches with the approbation of these Churches amongst whom we dwell. Besides, your Majestie needs not feare the bringing in of any novelties, rites, or ceremonies from us, who never did, or do intend, any such thing, specially since now all new Liturgy is interdicted us, not only by your Majestie but also by the States authority without which no new rites or ceremonies can be introduced.

Concerning the 4th. art. Howsoever we have just cause to thank God from our hearts for your Majesties religious care to have the truth maintained & error avoided: Yett we cannot a little wonder upon what ground or occasion your Majestie should be induced to suspect any such thing in us, among whom there is not a man that hath beene so much as tainted with any the least surmize either of Popery or Arminianisme, or any other erroneous sect in any point of doctrine; but ever have, still do, & through Gods grace allwayes shall stand strongly for the trueth established by the English & Dutch Churches. As for the 5th. art. We never thought nor conceived that your Majestys father of blessed memory intended any lesse power to us then is granted to the French in these provinces, Howsoever now (for what ends we know not) men would make your Majestie believe the contrary. And (as in our former declaration we have shewed) lesse we cannot have if we have any, even for the practising of these things which in this article your Majestie commends to our care, Neither hope we that your Majestie will seeke to diminish that our power; But such is our confidence That your Majestie will rather be a happy instrument to procure the continuance & ratification of the same unto us, which, if it shall be your Majestys pleasure to doe, we promise as your Majestys faithfull & loyall subjects to labour to the uttermost of our power to approve ourselves in all our proceedings to the Lords the States, & to all Churches, & to your Majestie in the particulars recommended unto us by this article. And thus we prostrate our selves att your Majesties feete in all humility, beseeching your Majestie to entertaine us in your Royall grace & favor, & not to conceive any the least un-duetifullnes in any of us, either towards your Majesty or the Churches of England & Scotland upon any report or informa-tion by such as happily may rather seeke the satisfying of particular mens humors then the respect either of Gods glory, or of your Majestys honor in the peace & wellfare of the Church. Att Rotterdam the 4th. of June, 1628.

VII.

Extract of a letter of instructions by King Charles I to Henry Vane, Ambassador to Holland. Westminster, No-vember ?, 1629.[22]

. . . Besides the publick business you have in charge from us, there is likewise occasion of Direction to bee given you in particular affaire lately moved unto us by John Forbes, minister to our Merchants residing at Delft, concerning our Subjects of all Sorts in those parts professing our Religion & having Ministers and Preachers in severall Congregations (for whom they desire convenient maintenance and to have them kept in good Rule and Covenant, without Scandall to the Church) wherein our Agent there can well informe you what passed in the King our Fathers time: how by his Authority the like liberty being granted them for convening and assembling as is used in the Walon Churches, they practised the same at first to good purpose for their better maintenance and Government of their Ministers; how they were carried soon after by some hot-headed Men amongst them to Courses contrary to the first good Intention, assuming to themselves power of creation of Ministers and of framing new Liturgies, or at least translating the Dutch Liturgy into English with intention to introduce the same amongst our Subjects; which caused us to forbid their further assembling, foreseeing the ill Consequence of such presumption. But in case, seeing their Errour, you find them (as Forbes doth assure they are) more moderate and temperate, and that they can hold themselves to the first intention of their meetings to see that no Schisms in Doctrine nor scandall in manners grow amongst them, without taking to them selves

22 *State Papers 16*, vol. 152, fol. 74 (Public Record Office, London). Briefed in *Calendar of State Papers, Domestic Series, Charles I, 1629-31*, 110.

the liberty of creating Ministers or framing new Liturgies or
translating the Dutch into English, and that they doe nothing
Cross or Contrary to our Church Government here in England,
wee like well you should give them all help towards their
maintenance and allow their meetings once yearly, so as they
ever give account in writing what passeth amongst them to
our Ambassadour or Agent, . . . according as they did the
first years after the King our Father procured unto them that
Priviledge.   Given under our Signet at our Palace of West-
minister. . . .

VIII.

Mr. Pagetts 20 Propositions to Mr. Hooker with his
Answere thereto.[23]

Question 1.   Whether it be lawfull for any to resort unto the
Publique Meetings of the Brownists, and to Communicate
with them in the WORD OF GOD?   Negatur.

Answer: To seperate from the faithfull Assemblies and
churches in England as noe churches is an error in Judgment
and sinne in practize held and mayntained by the Brownists
& therefore to comunicate with them, either in this their opinion
or practize, is sinneful & utterly unlawfull; but for a christian both their opinion & practize, to heare occasionally amongst
them & so to communicate with them in that part of Gods worde
(which I conceave to be the meaning of the first Quaere)
is not so farre, as I yet see simply unlawfull, but may prove
occasionally offensive if either by goeing, we should encourage
them to goe on in their course of seperation, or els by our
unwise expressions, might serve to weaken ours, to like of it
our selves, and so to drawe them to a farther approbation of
that way, then was before meet; whereupon it followes, if wee
give these occasions of offence wee sinne if wee do not abstaine,
but if these occasions of offence may be removed, by our constant renouncing of their course of the one side and by our
free and open profession of our intents on the other side, That
wee goe only to heare some savorie point opened, and to benefitt
by the guifts of some able Minister, that may come amongst

23 *Boswell Papers*, I, fols. 67-72. Endorsed [fol. 72 verso] ''20 Propositions by
  Mr. Paget Minister of the English Congregation at Amsterdam to Mr. Hooker
  with his Answer. 1632.''   Burrage publishes parts of the first three ''Propositions.''   *See, English Dissenters*, I, 304-305; II, 274-76.

them; if I say the giving of any Just offence by these or any
other meanes may be avoided, I conceive then it is not a sinne
to heare them occasionally, and that some men may prevent such
occasions, it is to mee, it is to mee [*sic*] a very disputable
question not having ever studied this point before.

Quaere 2.   Whether those Members of the Church which som-
tymes heare them & stifly maintaine a Libertie therein are to
be tollerated or rather censured?   Censured.

Response.   For the practice of members according to the
former caution & interpretation being taken up & mayntayned,
though stiffly, which Argumente because it is but questionable
and disputable, before they be fully convicted of their sinne,
they ought to be tollerated rather then censured; And this
moderation in things which are disputable, and not absolutely
necessary to salvation the Apostle enjoynes, Rom: 14: 1. 2. 3.
Heer also remember that the same degree of paines for convicting is not so sufficient in one disposition as another.

Quaere 3.   Whether such of the Brownists as have not re-
nounced their Seperation from the Church of England, Nor
yett allow Comunion with the Publique estate thereof, may
lawfullly be recommended for members of our church?
Negatur.

Response.   The not renouncing seperation from the faithfull
assemblies in England and the not allowance of comunion
with the Publique state of the church of England, This meer
opinion can in no wise make a man unfitt to be receaved a
member of this congregation, unlesse wee will say that such a
man (being in his judgment & life otherwise altogether un-
blameable) in Judicious charitie is not a visible Christian,
which is a more ridged censure then the wisest of the separation would give waie unto in a proportionable kinde, and I
suppose a pious hart dare affirme; and if in the judgment of
reasonable charitie he may be counted a member of Christ, and
so a saint, by the same charitie he may be counted fit to be
a member of a congregation, I Cor: 1. 2.   Besides, to judg
a man unfitt to be recommended for an irronious opinion in
such a kinde is to confirme the Brownists in that unsupport-
able and obsurd censure, which now they mayntaine touching
those who hold the churches in England true churches and

professe they will occasionally communicate therein for 'tis easie for them to inferre thus, if wee think them fitt to be members of a true church, who hold against the church of England. As equall reason (will they say) that wee shold think those unfitt matter for a true church who hold for the church of England since they judg that church to be as bad as any can judg theirse to be; so I judg of the 3 Quaeres.

Quere 4. Whether it be lawfull for Ministers to use set formes of Prayer, and to read them out of a book in the Publique worde of God? Affirmatur.

Response. Some sett forme of prayer may be used & read out of a booke by a Minister if he do it in a right season in a right measure after a right manner, so I affirme. But since there is no use of this in this church why it should be questioned I see not, unlesse men desire to finde differences of opinion.

Quaere 5. Whether in the Conclusion of other prayers you be content to use the Lords prayer before or after Sermon? Affirmatur.

Response. The Lords Prayer may be used, and as occasion serves I will use; but its confessed on all hands that its lawfull not to use it when wee pray; And therefore I will take myn owne liberty as I see fitt; The comissaires in England are contented with so much; & the most & best Ministers in the severall Diocesses do no more; Soe I affirme.

Quere 6. Whether Infants whose Parents are not Members of the church may be lawfully baptized according to the manner of the Reformed Churches?

Response. The manner how these churches do baptize such children whose parents are of no church, I do not by experience knowe, nor in this short time can tell how to iearne fully all the particular circumstances thereof; yet if it be such as I understand by Relation, I judge it unlawfull for mee to followe leaving the churches to their owne judgment; so I conceave.

Quere 7. Whether it be lawfull to Preach on festivall dayes, as at Christide, Easter, Whitsontide as is used in these Countries? Affirmatur.

Response. A Minister publique by professing against all superstition and popish holynes that is placed in dayes, and soe instructing the people, teaching also the liberty that people hath to labour and do their ordinary workes of their calling without scandall upon any of those dayes, which are not sabbathes, with these cautions and expressions, I judg it lawfull then to preach.

Quere 8.   Whether it be lawfull to use a Reader in publiquely in the Church which is no Minister? Affirmatur.

Response.   It is lawfull to use a Reader publiquely which is noe Minister; Soe I affirme.

Quere 9.   Whether comon and ordinary offenses are to be judged & determyned by authority of the Eldership without publique cognition of the Church?

Response.   This and the next Quaere is of so generall expression that they may admitt of an answere in a large manner sutable to the worde in generall, Though happily it will not afford a satisfactorie explanation thereof; but because it is only to be expected that my answere should be noe otherwise expressed then the question is propounded, it shall suffice to affirme some controversies, comon & ordinary offences, may be judged & determyned by the authority of the Eldership, without the publique cognition of the church; Some offences comon & ordinary in some cases, which may fall out, cannot be decided without publique cognition.

Quere 10.   Whether it be lawfull to receave any a Members into the church without publique examination of them before the whole Congregation? Affirmatur.

Response.   This 10th question admitts of a like answere to the former; Some members may be received without publique examination, and yet the case may so fall out that some cannot without publique examination.   This in generall to generall Quaeres; if they had bine more particularly propounded, They should have so bine answered.

Quere 11.   Whether a perticular Congregation have power to call a Minister without the Aprobation of the Classis under which they stand? Negatur.

Response.   Before I answere the Quere, I would aske one thing which might give a little light to that which shalbe said afterwards, namely how the first Classis that ever was upon the face of the Earth came to be constituted; and I conceave it cannot be denyed but that it was made by the combination

of severall Ministers & Elders, yea of Severall congregations,
wherein it must needes followe that those particular congregations had power from Christ to call a Minister, and so did by
that their power choose and call their Ministers fully & compleatly before there was a Classis; and therefore had not the
power derived from a Classis, or by but from the direct Ordinance and appoyntment of Christ, which power they may not
give away and none can take it away, being a legacy left them
by the Lord JESUS; as Doctor Ames disputes and determynes
in his 4th booke of cases of Conscience,[24] page 165. Touching
the Quere then my opinion is this, a particular congregation
hath compleate power by Christ his institution to give a compleate call to a Minister without any dirived power from a
Classis; They which had compleate and perfect Ministers
before any Classis had power fully to call them without any
Classis, but a particular congregation had perfect & compleate
Ministers, i. e., perfectly and compleatly called, before any
Classis, Ergo. Yet if by mutuall consent the congregation
hath combyned it selfe with the Classis, They shall doe piously
and expediently freely to crave the approbation of the Classis
That they may be more confirmed or, if doubts should arrise,
better directed in their course; alwaies provided that if the
said Classis should not approve, They may lawfully and without sinne choose, without or against the Aprobation of the
Classis, if they sawe good reason by the convenient fittness
of the party to induce them thereunto. And so I judg of the
11 Quere.

Quere 12. Whether Classis and Synod have authority not only
of admonishing and counsailing, but also of judging and decid-
ing the Controversies of Perticular Congregations? affirmatur.

13. Whether it be lawfull for a perticular Congregation to
excommunicate any offender whom they judg obstinate either
without or against the judgment of the Classis under which
they resort? Negatur.

14. Whether there be any superior Ecclesiasticall power to
censure or judg either a whole congregation or the greater
part thereof erring in matter of faith and religion, or whether

24 William Ames, *Conscience with the Power and Cases thereof* . . . First published
in Latin about 1632; translated and published at London, 1643, in *The Workes
of the Reverend and Faithful Minister of Christ, William Ames. Translated
out of Latine for publike use.*

in such a case, after admonition, their Soules are to be left
to the imeadiat Judgment of Christ and their bodies to the
Sword & power of the civill Magistrate? Prima pars affirmatur. 2da Negatur.

Response. These 3 Queres desire a large explacation if they
should be clearly and fully opened without exception, which if
I should doe, My answere would growe too tedious for me to
write in this short time, and may be for you & ther brethren
to read. Therefore shortly and playnly thus: In all of them
I concurre with the judgment of Doctor Ames the 4th booke
of his casses of Conscience, pages 179-180; of Mr. Parkar the
3 booke Ecclesiasticall Policie;[25] in severall passages of sundry
chapters from the 2 to the 14th of Mr. Bayns his Diocessans
Tryall,[26] page 13, conclusion 4, page 21; Wherein how farre
they differ from you, I doubt not but you fully knowe; And
this, I suppose, may serve or suffice for the present; yet if you
desire more particular expression upon notice I shall give it.

Quere 15. Whether the Church hath any power or Jurisdiction over him who, being privie to himselfe of any crime, doth
therefore of his owne accord depart from the communion of
the Church and holy things least he should be cutt of, and
whether such a one be to be left to the cyvill Magistrate, and
to others that have obtayned power over him by nature or law?
Prima Pars affirmatur; 2da Negatur.

Response. The scope of this Quere I do not fully understand
and therefore happily shall not give that present satisfaction
thereunto, But expresse what I perceave. The difficulty, as
farre as I can guesse, lies in these words, Being privie to
himselfe; 2. Departs of his owne accord; for it seeme to me to
imploye a fault which the church neither did nor could take
notice of, and therefore did not, nay could not, proceed against
him; if now he depart from the church, his owne heart mov-
ing him first thereunto, and got consent also from the congregation that he might so do becoming a member of another
church, if then his fault should be found out, I conceave the
church from whence he came having dismissed him & not
knowing at his dismission any offence against him, cannot

25 Robert Parker, De Politeia Ecclesiasticae Christe, et Hierarchica opposita
   (Frankfurt, 1616).
26 Paul Baynes, The Diocesans Tryall (London, 1621).

now proceed to lay any censure. The church hath only power of them who are members of the church. Besides, to what purpose should the church which he hath left Excommunicate him, when the church wherin he is a member ought to doe it & may be will; therfor, to them he is lost for Ecclesiastical censure and to the Magistrate for his corporall punishment if his fault so deserve; But if he shall wilfully depart & joyne him selfe either to no assembly or to a false one, The churches authority is not then evacuated by such dealing, and therfor they should proceed with him according to the order of Christ, & so either reforme him or censure him as such a fault & the expression of his impenitencie shall deserve.

Quere 16. Whether suspension from the Lords Supper maie be used in some cases as a lesser Excomunication? Affirmatur. Response. Suspension from the Supper may be used in some cases, soe I affirme & consent also.

Question 17. Whether it be lawfull for private Members of the Church to interpret the Holy Scriptures at such sett dayes and places where sundrie members of divers families ordinarily assemble together? Negatur.

Response. The answere of this Quere depends upon the explanation of twoe things: 1. What it is to interpret Scriptures.

2. Upon what grounds it may be done. To interpret Scripture is to judg aright of the sence & meaning of the words; and after to expresse our judgment to others and to cause them to understand. 2. This may be done from a double ground, partly from ex officio place of authority, which is conferred upon us by the church and by which wee have commission thus to interpret as teachers so appoynted.

2. This course of interpretation may arise ex dono from the guift that Christ doth dispence to severall members according to their measure and the place they hold in the body. And this Doctor Ames in his 4th book of his cases of Conscience Cap: 5, page 162, Disputes & concludes both by scripture and reason that it was the lawfull practise of all able Christians indifferent upon occasion to teach & in a right sence to preach the Gospell in all places privately as opportunity & expedience served, to which purpose he judiciously alleadgeth 8:14 & 11.19

& 18:24; so this being a duty founded in Christianity, as there he shewes, there needes noe publique approbation of the Church, to call a man hereunto, as the Church useth to call the officers, but only direction and information by the Minister of the Word and private advise as occasion serveth to teach men not to go beyond their gift; but, as they may use it lawfully, so must they looke into their particular practises that they do it expediently; and much lesse needs there any publique officer to goe along with them to moderate their actions in this kinde; but if there shalbe any miscarriage in this or any other Christian practise as any shall observe it who are present or others of the Church shall understand it, they are to deale with them brotherly, according to the rule sett downe by Christ for the reformation of sinne. Briefly then, if it be a Christian duty thus allowed by Scripture & practised by the saints to interpret the Gospell as opportunity serves occasionally, the same Christians still keeping the proportion of their gift, nor crossing their places, employments, & finding other expedients for the action, they may at sett tymes and in sett places doe it ordinarily, being an ordinary duty of all Christians, as the gifts, opportunities, expediences serve. If any other distempers accompany the persons, if they contemne the publique ministery, if they violate discipline, if they unlawfully joyne with any who are counted wavering Starres by Jude, and breake any rule of direction there delivered by the Sperit, if Wives disobediently demeane themselves towards their husbands, if lastly they dissemble, coloure over their courses, those I say & the like failings issue from the follies of mens mynds, the corruption of mens hearts; but are not caused from the practise of this Dutie, the cautions of Expedience order such like attended therein.

Quere 18. Whether in a Reformed Church it be lawfull for Ministers and People or divers families without publique authoritie to sett apart occasionall dayes of fasting and humiliation wherin they may meet together for Religious Exercises and to signifie the same unto Ministers and some families of other Congregations that they in like manner may do the same? Response. For Ministers so to meete as is specified, their ordynary particular occasions pressing thereunto, or extraor-

dinary necessities of the Church calling to them to fasting &
prayer, such meetings, I say, are not only lawfull but necessarie
in some churches; Nor is yet needfull that wee should expect
that publique authority should enjoyne this Christian private
dutie, no more then wee should looke that the Magistrates
should make a lawe to presse Christians to the communion
of saints before they should are to addresse themselves thereunto.

Quere 19. Whether true repentance or any saving grace go
before faith in those that are Regenerate? Negatur.
Response. There is a double repentance, the first of preparation, wrought by the Almightie and irresistable power of the
sperit causing the sinner to goe out of him selfe and sinne in
humiliation before he can goe to God in Christ by faith in
vocation, and this goes before faith; and I conceave it to be
nothing but the stroke of the Spirit in the very first work of
Conversion, wherein the soule hath it selfe meerly passive, &
as our Divines use to speake, and in the true nature of it,
cannot be in any Reprobate. 2dly. Ther is a repentance in
sanctification, that word being strictly so takene it comes after
faith, so Mr. Rogers of Dedham in his Treatise, so Mr. Chibale
[Sibbald] in his Treatise of the tryall of Faith.

Quere 20. Whether are wee justified by the Active as by
the passive obedience of Christ? affirmatur.

Response. Wee are Justified as well by the Active as by the
Passive obedience of CHRIST: And these are my poore
thoughts for the present touching all these Questions propounded, and as my judgment, so likewise my practise, is like to be
so farre as my Conscience calls me thereunto, giving wiser &
better then my selfe loving leave to think other & do other,
being ever willing to heare better argument and any convicting
Reason, & to stop thereunto; and because I do apprehend your
opinion & affection to be so farr setled that you conceave there
cannot be a peaceable concurrance in such distance of Judgment, I am resolved contentedly to sitt downe & sudainly as I
see my opportunity to depart, wishing the God of peace would
finde so comfortable an Assistant as may sute with you in all
truth & holynes for your mutual comfort and the Building up
of the bodie of CHRIST.

IX.

[Notes concerning the English Ministers, Churches, and the Congregational Classis in the Dutch Netherlands, c. 1621-1633. Probably prepared by Stephen Goffe for Sir William Boswell. 1633.][27]

Concerning the Classis:

That in the year 1621, Mr. [John] Forbes obtained a Commission for the English Classis. Mr. [John] Paget, & Mr. [Thomas] Potts refused to be members of it; And being pressed to come in, They made their case known to the Amsterdam Church Classis of which they were, & gave their reasons, which were so approved that the Classis made an Act That they thought it best the English should have no Classis, & that Mr. Paget & Mr. Potts should not be drawn from the Dutch Classis they were in. This Act, with the reason, are upon register & recorded. That Mr. Paget &c being yet further pressed by the English Classis, The business was presented to the North Holland Synod, where the former Act of the Amsterdam classis was Confirmed; this is likewise to be seene upon record.

Mr. Forbes notwithstanding this, once with Mr. [Thomas] Scott, the Utrecht minister, & another time with Mr. [Samuel] Batchelour, came to Amsterdam privately to the Burgomasters to desire them to constraine Mr. Pagett & Mr. Potts to be of their Classis. And the last time, which was with Mr. Batchelour, they went out of the towne and it was not knowne to Mr. Pagett nor any of the Dutch Ministers that they had beene there till afterward that the Burgomasters moved it to the Dutch ministers to deliver Mr. Paget &c. unto them. But afterward, & now at this present, the Burgomasters are so fully possessed with the unfittnes of Mr. Forbes project of a classis that they likewise joyne with the Ministers of Amsterdam to retain Mr. Paget from that English Classis.

That the two main reasons why the English Classis is condemned are these (as they may be seen upon record): 1. Because the Ministers of England which come over hither are of severall & inconsistent opinions differing from one another & from all reformed churches, as expressly that some are

27 *Boswell Papers*, I, fol. 146. Published in part in Burrage, *Early English Dissenters*, I, 296-97; II, 270-72.

Brownists, some Brownistically affected in particular opinions as: 1. in allowing private men to preach. 2. In denying formes of praior. 3. In admitting Brownists to their congregations not renouncing their Brownism. Some are Jacobites who require a New Covenant for members of a Church to make before they can be communicants. 2. Condemne the Discipline & Judging power of all Classes & Synods, & [hold] that they have only a power of consailing & advising, because every particular Congregation is a Church, and that a compleat church, and that it is Immediately given unto every Congregation from Christ to be a Single & uncompounded policy; (These are the very words of Mr. Jacob, & Parker, & Baines.)[28] And now the Dutch Classis & Synods conclude that such opinions as these do cleane overthrow the nature of their government; and that amongst such diversity of opinion no true Classis can be framed.

2. Because of the Complaint of the French & Wallons in these Countries, made because they have a Classis graunted unto them, It were better (they say by Experience) that they had no Classis, but were (as Mr. Paget is) mixed into the Dutch Classis, for by reason of the distance of their dwelling they can not have Monthly or quarterly Meetings, as Classes have, but only annuall as Synods; and that then there is such trouble in their gathering together, some dwelling in one province & some in another, at such great distance that they never all meet & by reason of their few meetings there grow up many Enormities in particular Congregations unpunished; which were they in the Dutch would be rapidly & oftener remedied. There be many other reasons given, but these were related unto me.

That now in this present yeare, 1633, Mr. Forbes & his Classicks obtaining a new Commission for their classis from the Councell of State, Mr. Paget hath presented the business againe to his Classis at Amsterdam the 4th of Aprill, being the first Monday in the month. And they have promised their utmost endeavour to hinder it; that they will press it to their Synod when it comes, & have delegates appoynted to the States to declar the compleat judgement of their owne & divers other classes & Synods against it.

28 Henry Jacob, Robert Parker, and Paul Baynes.

Concerning Mr. [Thomas] Hookers busines.

Stephen Oswood, an Inn Keeper dwelling neer the old Church at Amsterdam, wrote a Letter to Mr. Hooker presently upon the death of Mr. Potts. Mr. Hooker, upon his Invitation, promised to come, But must be *Caled;* he would but come first to Rotterdam, expecting the Call from hence. How Mr. Paget putt in to the Elders that unlesse Mr. Hooker were examined about his judgement in the points above, that he would not nor could not write for him, nor could he be chosen without hazard of the grace of that church; Notwithstanding the Elders (upon [Hugh] Peters his recommendations of him) put a *Call* for him without Mr. Paget.

In all his private discourse with Mr. Paget he avoided to speak of those poynts. Having leave to preach one afternoon, he would confute what Mr. Pagett had delivered in the morning (*Sc. That it was unlawfull for private members of a Congregation to preach*). Hereupon Mr. Paget was the more earnest to have Mr. Hooker declare himselfe.

At last he constrained the Elders to goe with him to demand his answers to certain points which brought forth those 20 Questions & Answers which you have seen. Which notwithstanding, the Elders were about to go on to choose Mr. Hooker. Wherefore Mr. Paget was constrained to put them into Latine & to present them & his case to the Classis, Who made it in an Act That a man holding those opinions could not be chosen pastor within the power of ther Classis & that so the Elders should desist.

Notwithstanding the authority of the classis (Mr. Hooker had taught them as you may see in his answers that they might go on), they were proceeding; so the Classis made the Synode acquainted with it, Who allowing the former Act & gave premptory Commands (by their delegates sent of purpose to the consistory) that they should chuse another. And then the Eldership obey, & so have *called* Mr. [Samuel] Balmeford, who now deliberates.

But now Mr. Forbes thinkes his part begins to help at a Dead Lift; so first he comes to Amsterdam to know the reason why Mr. Hooker Could not be chosen, pretending that the merchants of Delph were about to chuse him his Assistant; which yet to conceived ought not to be, if he were justly excepted against by the Dutch Classis. The Ministers of Amsterdam willed him to return and that when the classis was gathered he should have a letter to certifie each of their Exceptions against him; which by a letter accordingly was done, Subscribed by Hermann Antonider, pastor of Narden. Mr. Forbes not being satisfied with these Exceptions, writt an Expostulatory letter to the classis which they tooke very unkindly; & sent him back a sharpe answer reprehending his medling in things above his place, & plainly blaming the arrogancy of his spirit & though to blame Bishops himselfe [was] more then Episcopall. This letter was subscribed by Jacobus Laurenting, pastor of Amsterdam, & written by him. Mr. Forbes will not shew it, but if need be all these acts are easie to be produced and the copy of the Letters. And here Mr. Forbes is quiet; Except that as Mr. Deputy [Edward Misselden] tells me, he saith he will make the Classis repent it.

Concerning Mr. Peters Ordination.

1. There was a New Covenant made with certaine precise & strict obligations to which they should bind themselves. And he would be chosen by none but them that would put their hands to that paper. This, saith Mr. Paget, was a kind of Excommunication to above two parts of the Congregation in former times & hath caused the difficulty of administering the sacrement, because he will give it to none but them whose names are at his New Covenant. These New Covenanters must chose & call him. So before these a Sermon was made by Mr. Forbes.

2. There was χειροτονεία first by all the men: 'but,' said Mr. Forbes, 'I see what the men do, but what do the women do?' Thereupon they fell a χειροτον ising [!] too & lift up their Hands.

3. There was χειροθεσία The Imposing of all the hands of the present ministers except Mr. Day or who was not desired (*Mr. Grim of Weasell was present and confirms all this*) and Mr. Forbes held them above halfe an houre laying his burthen upon him in these words & manner, as if he had never been made Minister.

One Thomas Craford who doth usually eate at Stephen Oswoods is putting out the Bibles. They are printing in a house by the South Church, and one Stasmore, a Brownist, who is discontented about the business if it be well carried, will easily tell all & bring you to the place. Stephen Oswood is certainly the man which procured the printing of all the blew books, for he saith he hath 100 & 200 copies sent him of the bookes; Which cannot be if he were not extraordinary in the matter, & the other book binders confesse they buy them of him. And he denies not but that Mr. Hooker made the Lettres pattents; & if so then any man may see to [that] he made the Curtaine,[29] &c. Dr. Ames his fresh Suite against ceremonies[30] is quite done except the epistle & errata; the same Oswood procured the printing & can shew some of it done.

X.

The Chaplains Charg.[31]

You shalbe attendant in ministring of divine service & doing all things lawfull to the Governor, his lieutenant, or Deputy, & fellowshippe, as well in the Marts, as also in the townes of Bridges, Middelburg, & other places Where the said Governor or his Deputy shall assign you.

You shall also be diligent & ready to every person of the said fellowshippe in time of sickness & other necessity to give ghost [?] Counsell, as to your cure belongeth.

You shall not take upon you any charg of Executorshippe or Administration of the goods of any person of this fellowship whom it shall please God to take out of this transitory Life on this side of the seas, but by the advice of the Governor or his Deputy, or by the advice of the most honest, grave, & credible persons of the said fellowship in the towne or place where such case shall falle out; And forthwith shall give due & true information & report to the said Governor, or his Deputy of all such goods & debts as shall come to your knowledg, to the intent that the said goods & debts may be disposed of where they belong or ought to be bestowed of right.

If you shall know any manner of person or persons of evill rule or misguiding, you shall admonish & counsell him

29 Possibly refers to J. Henric, *The Curtaine of Church Power and Authoritie, in things called indifferent* . . ., published in 1632.
30 William Ames, *A Fresh Suit against Human Ceremonies in Gods Worship* (1632).
31 *Boswell Papers*, I, fols. 54-55. Endorsed (fol. 55 verso) "Orders concerning the Chaplen And acts of Court of Deputy & Company of Merchant Adventurers. *In Delf. 1631.*" Probably written by Edward Misselden.

to amendement; And if he do not, or will not by your counsell be admonished & amended, then you shall give knowledg thereof to the Governor or his Deputy to the intent that Reformation may be had.

Atque haec super urba Sacerdotis.

Other orders concerning the chaplain & the church, viz: The chaplain shall have his chamber or Lodging free in the English house, or in such place as shalbe appointed for him, together with an yearely alimentation & other fees & availes, as to the fellowship shall seme meet & convenient for his sustenance & reasonable entertainement.

No person of this fellowship shall play at any Game of Cards, tables, &c in the Conserg or free hosts houses upon the Lords or Sabboth day, upon paine of 5 shillings sterling. And the Conserg or free host, knowing thereof & suffering such play or game, shall forfeit & pay 10 shillings sterling to the use of the poore.

No person of the fellowship shall shew, sell, or deliver any clothes, kersies, or other wares or merchandize whatsoever on the week dayes in time of publique divine service or Exercise, upon paine of 20 shillings sterling. Neither shall any person shew, sell, or deliver, or buy, barter, or bargen in way of merchandize on the Sabbath or Lords day, or other day set apart or appointed for a generall fast, or thanksgiving unto God, though other wise the said be a shew day, upon the same penalty of 20 shillings sterling to the use of the fellowship without favor or pardon.

Whosoever of the fellowship shall separat himself from the church or congregation established by the common consent of the fellowship on this side of the seas according to their priviledges, such persons, upon his separation plainly discovered, shall be first called before the Governor or his deputy & the Assistents or Associats in presence of the pastor or minister of the Congregation then in place; And if after admonition to him there given he shall not reunite himself to the same church & behave him self as a member thereof ought to doe, order shall forthwith be taken for the sending away & shipping into England of such person.

Generall Court held in Delft last of October, 1631. Whereas it hath bene observed by some of the Assistents that at the last Election of Elders & deacons divers handicrafts men and others unfree of this fellowship were admitted as members of the Congregation to have their voices with the brethren of the Companie in the said Election; which is conceived to tend to the prejudice of the priviledges granted to this fellowship on that behalf. And therupon the orders concerning the chaplains charg being read & examined, it was thought meet & resolved that Mr. Deputy be entreated to confer with Mr. Forbes & the Elders & to look back what order & direction they have Received from the Companie for the governement of the church, & to let the Companie have a copie thereof to the end they may consider of them; & in case they finde any Inconvenience by them in these times they may consider how the same may be redressed.

Generall Court in Delft, 12 November, 1631. Mr. Deputy signified that he had had some conference with Mr. Forbes about that which past at the last court concerning unfree men which were made equall in their votes at the last Election of Elders & Deacons with those of the companie & which the Companie conceived to trench upon their governement & priviledges, & therefore held the same altogether unfit. Whereunto that Mr. Forbes gave him for answere that he was of the same opinion with the Companie & that he had already given order to Hen. London to give notice unto such men to forbeare in that kind hereafter; Which the said Mr. Forbes signified him self, being sent for to this court, & promised to take care thereof for the future. But for that which passed further, concerning the order of the last court, it was thought meet that nothing should be recorded.

Generall Court in Delft, 26 December, 1631. Mr. Deputy signified that according to the passage of the last Court concerning the church governement, he intended to have let the matter rest, but that since that time Mr. Forbes & the Elders had desired a conference with him, which being held betwixt them, accordingly his worship found that things were very much aggravated, & Construed otherwise then they were meant; That he is well content that they shall have that respect which is due unto them; That the occasion was not given by himself, but proceeded from their owne Act about the choosing of the Elders & Deacons; That he read that paper or writing to the minister & Elders which he would have read at the last Court, wherein he collected somthing for the information of his owne judgment concerning the office of Elders; but lest the Companie to be informed by [edge of page gone] Mr. Forbes, whose office it was so to doe; That he hath gone over the whole Scripture to find out the name & use of Elders, which Signify two things: either a man of age, or a man of office. For age, if the Elders of this times were understood men of wisdome, & of good life & Conversation, then the name was well given; But as an office, it is given to none but such as are instituted by God, as Apostles, Bishops, Pastors, & teachers. That somthing was spoken to him by the Elders as if he went about to alter the course they now are in, & to have the Church governed by the Governor or his Deputy & Assistents; but he ment no such thing, but that the governement may be continued as it is, & in those persons, & that there must be discipline, order, & policy in the church; That he needed not to have spoken so much, but that it was desired by the Minister & Elders; That it had grieved him much that, being in authority, the minister & Elders never advised with him in anything concerning the church; but that now they have promised to hold a loving correspondence with him; & therefore he wished the Companie to give all respect & reverence to them in their places, as he for his part should be also content to give them, being content to rest in the thing as it was left between him & the Elders.

After which relation, it was thought meet that this question should be propounded to the Companie: whether the governement of the Church should continue as heretofore, without any chang? Which being done accordingly, the court resolved, that the Governement in the Church hitherto used shall continue so without alteration.

XI.

[Edward Misselden's Notes on the English Churches in the Low Countries for the English Privy Council, 1632.][32]

THE ABUSES

That there are about 25 or 30 English Churches in the Lowe Countries, which for the most part are Seminaries of

32 *State Papers 16*, vol. 224, fol. 57. Public Record Office, London. Briefed in *Calendar of State Papers, Domestic Series, Charles I, 1631-33*, 432.

disorderly preachers.   And albeit, that some men may think that the Land's well quit of them, for that they are beyond the seas, yet there they do more harme then they could do here:

In or by {
Corrupting our Nation
writing scandalous books
holding continuall Correspondence with the
Refractories of England.
}

That the Marchants-Adventurers preachers in the Low Countries are the chief of those Refractories there. That some of them opposed King James in Scotland, & for which they were banished thence; yet continue the same opinions in the Low Countries, getting some kind of protection of the States. They will observe no formes of prayer, nor admitt of any Liturgy or divine service which is that *Cultus Dei* which ought to be in every Christian church; They will observe no solemnities, as Xmas day, the passion day &c, nor will they administer the Sacraments in any forme but their owne. They take upon them to plant churches & ordaine ministers; & have very much Laboured with His Majesty here & the states there to have an English Synod, on faire pretences but false grounds, & to serve their owne turnes.

That our preachers have not administered the Communion almost this 12 monthes, but did since that I, out of the care & duety of my place, have admonished them, they have refused it & made a great faction in the Company & persuaded them not to communicate with me nor accept me for the Companies Deputy; although I am Re-elected by the chief Court at Hamburgh with the consent of the Company here at London, & taken my oath in my place at Delft. Whereupon the Company here are forced to send over Commissioners with me to Examine these insolencies & to confirme me in my place: which are Mr. Law, their Deputy; Mr. Stymer, their Secretary; & Mr. Edwards, Lately their Treasurer.

☞ By which faction at Delft, against His Majesties Government there, may be guessed as by a true Scantling, what these of their mind would do against His Majesties Government here if they durst.

That the principall of this faction at Delft are such as have maried Duch wives, Expressly forbid by His Majesties charter on paine of disfranchisement for

{
His Majesties losse of his Subjects:
Their Corruption in Religion:
Their disclosing the secrets of our
    Country . . . [torn].
}

That all the rest are young men, which (for want of age & Experience) for Government whereby our trade of cloths away is almost thrust into [?-torn] the hands of the Duch.

THE REMEDIES

That the States admit of none of our preachers there, which have not subscribed to the Church of England; as themselves do not admit any of their owne which have not subscribed to their owne Church. And the inducement is strong, because His Majesty doth not admit or patronize any of their preachers here which oppose the States Governement. At least, that they be held to the States subscription, which many —ours especially—refuse. But no Synod by any meanes.
☞ Vide, States Subscription.

That if our Merchant Adventurers preachers which are leaders to the rest will submit to His Majesties Ecclesiasticall Government & to the Companies Governement in the affairs of our owne church & give due respect to me their Deputy-Governor, & reduce the Company there to peace & Love & obedience & reverence to their Governors & so administer the Communion, that they be continued in their places; otherwise that the Merchant Adventurers be enjoined to send over other reverend, learned, & conformable Divines in their roomes to recover our Company out of the these grosse absurdities.

That an Effectual Letter be written immediately to Mr. Boswell to have a carefull Eye to these things, to Countenance me the Deputy in this service to His Majesty & the Church; to assist those Commissioners now sent over; & if that their preachers & this faction at Delft cannot be reformed by the authority of the Company, that Mr. Boswell may use the Authority of the Lords & the names of these that resist to be certified over to the Lords.

That they be held to the plaine words of His Majesties Charter of disfranchisements; or if that [be] too hard, then instead of 20 ndks [?], for which they now get Letters of Indemnization, they may pay 500 ndks or pounds to the King to be restored to the Companies freedome, which is His Majesties graunt; which wilbe a good restraint of them & preservation of our trade from the Dutch.

☞ That the chief Governement of the Company be only Entrusted to the Company at London, according to former direction of the Lords. And that the Governor & Deputies be henceforth chosen at London for this & the forreine Courts; And that some grave & discreet men be sent over from hence at times convenient to Assist the Governement beyond the Seas, as anciently hath bene accustomed.

That so the Governement, which is a gemme of the kings crowne, may be maintained in its owne honor. And then even Strangers, *quasi Ex ungue Leonem*, will know the Soveraigne at home by the Subject abroad if meet governed. And if for this there need [be] a new Charter, they may renew their old, as they were [? torn] wont at the [change of every King (? torn)].

[Memorandum on reverse, by Secretary Windebank.]

29 Oct., 1632

Mr. Misselden, Deputy Governor of the Merchant Adventurers at Delft. Affronted in his government by some factions of the Company for his desire to conform them to the divine service of the Church of England.

That Company the seminary of such as oppose the government of the Church & state here.

Why his Majesties subjects though living in forain partes should not live in obedience to the government of the Church & State in England.

A letter to Mr. Boswell in favor of Mr. Misselden to assist him against those factious people & to compose those differences if he can; if not, to advertise the State here of the persons refractory.

To call the Governor of the Company before the Lords & to admonish him to look to those factions.

To threaten the calling in their charter in default of reformation.

To have a speciall eye to those that marry dutche women that they be called home again upon perill of forfaiting their estates here, that the King may not lose his subjects.

That the chiefe government of the Company be from henceforth at London, & not at Hamborough (as it is now) & that the governor & deputies be chosen here & not there.

The ancient of the Company refuse to go there, but sende theire apprentices & factors, which being young & inexperienced cause all this schisme.

The Charter howsoever to be renewed, as it hath ever bene at the change of every King; this having not yet bene renewed since his Majesties comming to the Crowne.

XII.

Nature & grownd of the Differences between Mr. Misselden, Deputy, & the Merchants of the Companie of Adventurers in Delft concerning Ecclesiastique affaires. 10 February, 1632/33[33] [A Memorial by John Forbes and his Elders to the English Privy Council.]

The true nature, state and ground of the trouble raised by Mr. Deputie Misselden in the Church of the Companie of Marchand adventurers in Delph.

1. Mr. deputie, after divers privat attemps, did at last openly set himself against the forme and order of ecclesiasticall government established and practised in this church by mutuall consent of bothe States from the first founding of this church untill now, that Mr. Misselden hath opposed it and laboured to overthrow and utterly to abolish it as unlawfull and contrarie to the word.

2. The governement that he labours to bring in place therof is such as hath no precedent in any church whatsoever; for he claimeth to himself, and that ex officio, as deputie, the whole and sole power of ecclesiasticall governement in this church as well as civill in the companie.

To make knowne to all that this is the truth of the controversie, we set down his own grounds maintained by him both by word and wryting, which are drawn partly from the

33 *Boswell Papers*, I, fols. 89-90.

nature of his office, as deputie governour, partly from the nature, as he interpreteth, of the governement established here in this Church, which he opposeth; and partly from the nature, as he fancieth, of this church different from all other churches.

1.   Touching the nature of his office first he resteth much upon the name of governour, or governement, esteeming that by that name he is made to have authoritie ex officio over the church and pastor in ecclesiastick affairs And government, as well as civill over the companie; being, as he alleadgeth, an Elder, or ecclesiasticall governour ex officio by vertue of his oath to the companie; and for confirmation hereof, he maketh his oath to the observation of the companies orders to bind him to the execution of all ecclesiasticall disciplin in this church, and none but him.   His reason openly professed was this, because he acknowledgeth no other ecclesiasticall lawes to be in this church *but the companies orders*.

2.   That this his devised authoritie might stand, he did maintain first, that he was an Elder ecclesiastick ex officio. 2. That there were no ecclesiastick elders, but such as preached. 3. That an elder and a bishop were all one, without any difference; wherupon this conclusion must follow, that the deputie must be ex officio the bishop of this church as well as deputie of the companie.   These things were publickly and obstinatly maintained by him against Mr. Forbes in a full assembly and court of the companie.   The bishops of Ingland may here sie, whether it be for them or himself that he stryveth.

3.   His second ground is taken from the companies orders before ever they had any allowance of a church or publick ministrie, and, as would appear, in tyme of popery, at what tyme the deputie had a domestick chaplen ordained by the companies orders to attend upon the deputie.   Hereupon he concludeth, that even the companies publick minister now under the gospell must in all matters concerning church governement only attend the deputies will and suffer him to take order with all things, nothing belonging to the minister but the letter only, putting no difference betwix a privat chaplen in a familie and a publick minister of a congregation.

4.   His third ground is taken from the conscience of his place and (as he is bould to say) Mr. Forbes his opposition to the

Kings governement, alleadging that it was proper to his place; so that if he had bene the author of that motion to have called such a church governement in question, it had bene verie lawfull, and answerable before god and man, and bouldly affirming, that that deputie which should know these things and others named by him, and suffer them, were aither insufficient in judgment or unfaithfull in his place. Thus still he draweth all authoritie both ecclesiasticall and civill to himself only by vertue of his place and office. Let here be marked whether every civill governour hath not by this rule appertaining to him, and that by his office, all authoritie ecclesiastick within his precinct? Where then are bishops, and in other churches, consisteries, Synods &c?

The ground from the governement ecclesiastick established and practised in this church of both states, is this:

1. That this ground is absolutely unlawfull and contrarie to the word of god; and to make this ground to hould, he layeth heavie reproaches and odious scandals upon it and Mr. Forbes and the Elders in standing for it. First, that Mr. Forbes and his Elders encroach upon the Kings governement given to the companie and endevour to maintain a Presbyteriall governement and disciplin above the Kings governement. 2. that Mr. Forbes and the Elders trench upon his Majesties governement and goe against our mother church in maintaining and abetting a schismaticall kynd of government. These scandals shew aither miserable ignorance of the nature of ecclesiasticall and civill governement, or malicious prophannes, or prophane malice.

The ground from the nature of this church is this; and it clears his former meaning and gros ignorance.

I. That this church is more eminent and of greater excellencie then any other church, and therfore is to be governed in another manner then any other church. This ground did the deputie publickly maintain before the full assemblie of the companie against Mr. Forbes.

Hereby all men may see that the deputie stryveth not for any disciplin established in any other church; but for a strange one, in his judgment more excellent then any established in any church; and (as shall appear) it is this, that this church be governed by him and no other. In which governement I leave to all men to consider, what is the supereminent excellencie answering the supposed excellencie of this church above others; as also, what honour he doeth to his mother church, as he calleth it, the reason wherupon he groundeth this, is this:

1. That the companie represents the King, and their governement is the Kings governement. He formeth the first two parts of this reason in a letter of his own thus; the companies governement is the Kings governement, but the King is supream governour over all persons and in all causes as well ecclesiasticall as civill. The contension I leave it to every mans collection, although he doth himself in that same letter gather it verie plainly.

In this argument proving the excellencie of this church above all other churches, first, I will not nominat the absurd prophannes therof; but I would demand, if there be any governement in the Kings dominions, in any citie, place or province, which is not the Kings; if all be his, what greater excellencie is there in the Companies governement then in all the rest; secondly, I would demand of Mr. deputie why, amongst his other reproachfull calumnies against Mr. Forbes, he accuseth him that he opposeth the governement of bishops as not of devyne institution; for aither this must be the deputies own opinion, or then he must esteem the governement that is jure divino to be more base in ecclesiasticall affairs then that which is jure humano; for I doe not think that he will say that he is jure divino ecclesiasticall governour of this church. Let both his Majestie and bishops sie what this man ayms at, which in all reason can be nothing els but to take to himself the same supremacie in the Company which is his Majesties Royal prerogative in his dominions, and so in effect to raigne as King in this Company.

Out of these things men may perceive wherin standeth the excellencie of this church above others in his judgment.

1. In that this church is not be governed by any minister of Christ designed and ordained by Him in his Word for ruling of His sanctuarie; but by the deputie or governour of the companie, and so not by any man having his authoritie and calling from Heaven or from Christ; but by a man, who hath

his authoritie and calling from men, even the Company of marchand adventurers, nay I may justly say and maintain, by a man having no calling aither from God or man to this office of ecclesiastick governement, but in proud prophannes usurped by him. 2. In that this church is not to be governed by any lawes of Christ, or His Word, or any decrees of counsels, or ecclesiasticall canons of any church whatsoever, popish or reformed, no not of Ingland; nor yet by the lawes of King or State; but only by the privat orders of the Companie made by them for ordering themselves in the priviledges of their marchand trade.

The summe of all commeth to this:

1. That Mr. deputie hath opposed the lawfull governement of this church lawfully established by mutuall consent of bothe States and accordingly practised since the first founding of the said church in Antwerp; and seecketh to have it abolished as unlawfull and contrarie to the word of God.

2. That the disciplin which he seecketh to establish in place therof is such as hath no example in any church whatsoever becaus he chalengeth the whole authoritie and power of ecclesiastical governement in this church to himself, and that ex officio as deputie, affirming that by his oath taken as deputie to the company he is charged not only with the civill governement of the company, but also with the ecclesiasticall governement of the church, defending that he is an Elder ex officio.

3. That he hath openly and professedly maintained that he acknowledgeth no other ecclesiasticall lawes in this church but the companies orders; so that neither the lawes of Christ, nor decrees of Counsels, nor canons of any church, neither any law of King or State hath any place in the ecclesisticall governement of this church, but only the orders made by the company for their trade, by his assertion.

4. That he doth affirme that nothing doth belong to the minister but the letter; and in all other things he is to attend upon the deputies will and to informe him of all misorders, as he who only hath power, with the assistants, to redres all scandals, yea even in some cases deserving excommunication.

5. That he hath contemned the authortie of the minister and

Elders, refusing to acknowledge their authoritie in ecclesiasticall matters, accompting no more therof then of boyes that
were in the streets.

XIII.

Extract out [of] Mr. [Edward] Misseldens Letters
Purposed to the Company of Merchant Adventurers in
London, March, 1632/33 st. vet.[34]

What concerneth the authority of my place. Our Minister
is & ought to be subordinat to the Company & so say our
orders & Constitutions for which to execute I have so often
take mine oath; but besides I have a Speciall commission bear-
ing date the 5th of July, Anno 1623, under the hands of the
Governor, Deputy, & the principall of the company to use the
authority of my place in repressing scisme, faction, & dissordre
in the Church, & in looking to the orders thereof. Whereby
ex officio I am bound not only to reprove but also to reforme
what is amisse.

But if I had none of these warrants, yet the very name
& nature of government doth call upon me therein to honor
the King & our Mother Church, & in both this ancient famous
fellowship. Or if I were no Governor but a meere member of
our Church & company, Or were it any of your cases, as privat
men, with what conscience could you subscribe to such a Church
government so contrary to His Majesties government & our
Mother Church, as is *neither conformable to the Church of
England, Nor the Reformed Churches of these Countries, nor
to the Church of this City where wee reside? That hath neither
Liturgie, Catechisme, confession, set formes of prayer, celebration of the Sacraments in any sett forme, exercise of the Lords
prayer, solemne thankesgivings for the birth & death of
Christ &c?* The wants of all which not only tend to the corrupting of our yong merchants which are sent out hither for good
education, but to cause strangers that looke upon us to think
that the church of England is as ill governed at home.

---

34 *Boswell Papers*, I, fol. 124. Endorsed on the reverse side: "Extracts of Deputy
Misseldens Letters, March, 1633, concerning Church at Delf &c."

XIV.

Dispatch to Secretary [John] Coke. Extra. The Hague, 8/18 March, 1632/33. [By] William Boswell.[35]
Right honorable.

My presents coming along with our former of the same date in awnswer unto severall parts of your Honors last of Feb. 15, concerneth our English Ministers & Church affayres in these parts; Which at my first entry & view I spied to be a spider of divers thrids, uneven, very much entangled, & requiring tyme to cleene them handsomely for his Majestyes honor & service without raysing of dust in my owne or others Eyes. But your Honor knowing best what wayes to direct, I shall faythfully applye myselfe accordingly as I have allready begunn. Wherefor, first for the English Church of the Merchant Adventurers in Delft. Imediately uppon receipt of your Honors Comaunds I spake with Mr. Forbes, Minister thereof (whom I presume Your Honor hath seene in England), & having divers tymes synce his retourne out of Germany (which was in January last) considered togither with him the differences betweene him & the Deputy (Mr. Misselden) concerning their Church, but without hope, or power to reconcile the same, I now playnely tould him that his Majestie had taken a resolution (as he had reason) in his owne Peculiars, to exempt Societies of his Subjects so immediately depending uppon him to have Divine Service performed according to the Lawes of his owne Church & Kingdome; And that I should be very glad to see him, a mann of gravity & creditt amongst our English Ministers in these Countries, beginn an Example of so good a worke. Whereunto he answered, That he knewe too well his duty to God & the King to oppose his Majestye or speake agaynst his purpose herein, adding that his age did call uppon him to retire & rest, which he purposed to doe, & meant very speedily to acquaynt the Company therewith that they might provide an other in his place. Synce then I have intimated as much unto the Deputy & some of the Company, in whom I doe not discover any intention to decline his Majestys Comaunds, though I perceyve a great affection in them unto their present Minister. I purpose within fewe dayes to speake with them

35 *Boswell Papers*, I, fols. 116-19.

together; But I must take leave to present unto your Honors consideration whether it be not necessary, before such comaundments doe come to be putt absolutely in execution, First to have the place fayrely voyded of Mr. Forbes, & how? 2. To provide another Minister conformeable to our Church? & how the Company who will pleade ever to have had their owne Election may be satisfied? 3. To settle this Ministers meanes, which doth arise partly from their Common Treasury (about 50 ld per annum) but more from their voluntary contributions. 4. To determine what course shalbe held with delinquents in Cases of Ecclesiastical Cognizaunce & Judgement? Whether power thereof shall wholly be kept in England, which would be very tedious, uncertayne, & scarce practicable, Or comitted to the Governor alone, which, perhaps, will not be so proper & safe? Or left unto the Governor and Company, of whom many are young Menn, & others carelesse, so that Censures for offences & scandalls will not readily be judged, It may come to be their owne Case? Or left in the Minister, Governor, & Assistants in the forme of a Consistory, who may regulate themselves & others of their Congregation to the same effect they now doe? To deferr the Introduction of our Lytourgie unto the Removeall of their Residence, yf any change of their place be so soone intended? 6. To make the Company of London sensible hereof, uppon whom these here, being most of them young Menn & factors for others, doe depend. That whosoever he be that comes in to be Minister may be a Mann of good worth, learning, & discretion to uphould the honor of our Church in this change, which wilbe very remarkeable & an Object of much expectation & envye, if not of opposition & heate by some of the States. It pleased my Lords of the Councell by their Letters in November last to require mee, among other services, to certifie the Constitutions of this Church, whereof I send the Report hereinclosed. By which your Honor may perceyve how strangely it hath hunge now above fifty yeares betweene the Church of England and the Reformed of these parts, tanquam in Inter-Mundijs Epicuri, clearly conforming it selfe neyther to the constitutions of the one nor the other, eyther for discipline, or for the parts, Order, & formes in Divine Service.

Your Honors Letters unto the Lord Vere, Coronell Morgan, & Coronel Herbert were presently delivered, as appeares by their awnsweres which come unto your Honor herewith. And that the whole story of the Buissines may appeare unto your Honor as it hath risen, May it please your Honor to knowe that the last Sommer one Mr. [Stephen] Goffe (a Mann of very good learning, & other wayes much deserving, my Lord Veres Chaplayne) by leave and Order of his Lordship, having begunn divine Service with some fewe prayers out of our Common Prayer Booke uppon Sondayes & some other dayes in the Regiment, Mr. [Samuel] Bacheler, Minister unto Coronel Morgans Regiment, being much scandalized thereat, came unto Goffe, & very much blamed him for doeing as he had without advising first with his Fellow Ministers; as yf it had byn a sinne to performe his dutye without asking leave of them who compted it noe sinne to neglect their owne. Notwithstanding, Goffe continued as he had begunne; & after his coming hither, the Army retourned out of the field, he petitioned to the Counsell of State for his Acte, & enterteynement, But was refused uppon some suggestion that he had done something prejuidiciall to these Reformed Churches; which he denying & justifyeing the same under his hand, he had both Act & Enterteynement delivered him, but with a clause in his Act (not inserted in any of his predecessors Acts) that he should never doe anything contrary, or innovate any thing in the Reformed Belgige Churches, uppon peine of being cashiered for the same; which doth not binde him from proceeding with our Prayers as he was resolved to doe, It being propre and necessary for our English Souldiers, part of the Ministers duty, & no hazard or innovation in these Churches. For they have ever byn read in one of our Regiments, now Sir Phillipp Pakenhams, heretofore the Lord Viscomte Wimbledons, by the Minister, And in all the rest by the Clerke of the Band, or some other appoynted to it, in the Ministers absence both in the Field & in Garrison publiquely without imputation of innovation, or Suspition of hazard, & prejudice to these Churches, without whose spher it may allso be rightly supposed that our Regiments are. Mr. Sclaer (borne in the Palatinate, sonne to a very faythful servant of the late King of Bohemia & Minister to a Coronells Regiment), hath shewed Mee a Licence (where-of I send your honor Copie), given him Anno Dei 162 [*sic*] by the Lord Bishop of Bristol to preach through that Diocesse, at the graunt whereof he was conformable to our Churche, as he still professeth himselfe to be with all duty and reverence, & protesting that he never opposed the Comon Prayer Booke, nor any way reprehended what Mr. Goffe had done, sayeing likewise that he will ever obey his Coronells Comaunds in the use of our prayers; which uppon his owne, & Coronells request, I have taken leave to signifie That the poore Mann may be exemped from wayting uppon your Honor, yf it may be; If it may not be, he promised to come uppon your Honors next call. Bacheler, Coronel Morgans Minister, a miserable poore Mann, I feare falleth into worse wayes, having byn with mee & shewed no great inclination to Conformity, but apologies for his comming to Mr. Goffe in the Army, & protestation that he never complayned against him any farther; What he will doe his Coronell will give your Honor accompt.

Your Honors Comaunds concerning the English Classis encountred with an Act of the Counsell of state reviving a former Act of A. D. 1621 (whereof I send your Honor Copies, & Translate herewith). Uppon my first knowledge thereof, understanding that Mr. [John] Forbes of Delft, [Hugh] Peters of Roterdam, & [Samuel] Banford [Balmford], Min-ister of our English Church here in the Hague, had byn with the Counsell of State, which I conceyved to be for some crosse caper. I presently sent for Forbes to knowe what they did & how they came thither? He sayed that every of them had severall Letters to appeare, which doeing they were asked why they did not execute their Commission granted (A. D. 1621)? [*sic*] for keeping the English Ministers in better Order. They awnsured that they had byn hindred by the Belgic Churches (2.) opposed from England (3.) devided among themselves (4.) and not encouraged, or assisted by their Lordshipps; after which, being commaunded to proceede a newe according to that Commission, they asked the Counsells order & Seale, which accordingly was delivered them. After this I asked him yf division among themselves (not above halfe submitting to their Classis) 2. opposition of the Reformed Belgige Churches, under whose wings they shelter themselves, and 3. the displeasure of his Majestie (who could not but thinke himselfe affronted by so insolent a combination) were not sufficient arguments to keepe a Mann (who had not lost his Witts) from affecting so unnecessary & yet troblesome an office? After which, having tould Me many things of my Lord of Dorchesters procuring and assisting in the passing of that Comission of 1621, And my ballancing that with his Lordshipps cryeing downe of the same before his leaving this place, & layeing to him the inconveniences which would fall uppon their owne heads yf they should proceed, he promised that they would attend the Councell of State agayne with petition not to be offended if they did forbeare to execute their Order untill they should have sought & knowne his Majestys liking thereof, which I presume they have done. The like discourse I held with Banford [Balmford] who liveth here very orderly, & diligent (without any offense I cann understand of) or affectation of such ymployement as some buysie bodies putt uppon him. Uppon this occasion I would humbly entreate your Honor to cause the Kings Printer to send Mee halfe a dozen, or a dozen, of our Common Prayer Bookes in French to bestowe among the States or others; for the Latine Impression is sould off, & none to be found newe; And yf your Honor so thinkes good to see in my Lord of Dorchesters Letters (of Dec. & January 1621.) how this act for the English Classis came to passe, and by his other Letters what particular directions King James gave him for suppressing the same, which I have heard were very punctually directed. Your Honor wilbe pleased to respitt Mee with favor for fuller awnswers to your Instructions concerning these Buysinesses untill my next, which wilbe very shortyly; I cannot learne that there hath byn any Classis, or Synod, of our English Ministers in these parts these 18. monthes past. Which is all your Honor shalbe trobled withall at present from—

Your Honors

Most humble & faythfull Servaunt
William Boswell.

XV.

Letter by Stephen Goffe to William Boswell.   Leiden,
March 10, 1633. n.s.[36]

Worthy Sir.

This day Mr. Sclatz tooke a jorney of purpose to Leyden
unto me, and his arrant was, first to find out whether I had
beene any informer against him; To which I answred that they
all did me wronge who thought I was any way active against him
or any others.   For I was very much grieved that there owne
doings had cast them into any danger.   And my opinion was
for his part that if he would be a tractable and conformable
man no doubt he would find frends to mediate for him, that
all may be made well.   Upon which he told me that he was
conformable and that he had Subscribed in England, and lived
according to his Subscription, & would againe do the same if
he were required.   But that his feare was the States would not
suffer him to read prayers, and that they would confirme the
English Classis.   For, Said he, I have promised to my Colonel
conformity & ergo a request hath beene put up to the States
for my Act; but the States wil not grant it, unlesse there be an
attestation from the classis.   Whereupon an attestation was
gotten from a Dutch classis (which I saw) and yet his act was
not granted because it was not from the English Classis.   Now
here stands the busines and ergo his jorney to me is mainely to
know what I will do with my selfe concerning this English
classis.   I tell him the English classis is a thing I understand
not.   But my councell to him was that he should refer himselfe
wholy unto Your selfe who is the kings Agent and unto his
owne Colonel: and to make knowne his tractablenes unto you,
& get some frends unto you that you would be pleased with your
good opinion of him to salve this mischeife.   And as for the
States and our Agent and Colonel to let them do their busines
amongst themselves, that for us ministers it was our duty
to be quiet, and be good Subjects to the king.   He thanked
me for my councell, but in fine he intimated that he was so
much Engaged to the Delph Classis (so he called it) that
he could not wel tell how to come off; that his Colonel was

---

36 *Boswell Papers*, I, fol. 107.   Endorsed, verso: ''Goffe.   10 March, 1633—
    Leyden.''

resolved to have him conforme, & that he knew they would never lett him; and that they now dealt more earnestly with the States then ever. I hope your power with this man wil bring him to a good sober sense. But certainely Sir *Morsus morientis sunt acertissimi* this now dying classis will at this time use all their force, & I see plainly the States are and wilbe more and more filled with prejudice against our church, and me in particular. As Dr. Wallens told me, Mr. Arsen, one of the Curators (they having occasion to speake of me) said, that he thought I ought to be looked unto, for that I was desirous to bring in those things which might trouble their church. This speach of My heer Arsen was told me twice which if you thinke fitt to speake of to Dr. Rivett who once offred me to go unto him—Mr. Sclatz told me further that they of Delph would not call their classis this 6 weeks because they must have time to write about and to send unto frends. He was not willing to be free with me; but you will heare all from him. I wondred he had not beene with you, but he saith he hopeth his colonel wil bring him to you. If this man were delivered from the inticement of those others of delph &c he would be brought a sober sense. This having happened this day I made bold to acquaint you with it. And thus with my humble service I rest

Your humblest servant
Stephen Goffe.

XVI.

William Laud, Archbishop of Canterbury, to Sir William Boswell. Lambeth, December 11, 1633.[37]

Worthy Sir,

I thanke you for all your love & respects to me & the great expressions which your Letters make of them. All

---

37 *Papenbroek MSS 2* (L), unpaged. Library of the University of Leiden, Holland. Two other letters from Laud to Boswell of a later date (Lambeth, May 29, 1639, and Croyden, Sept. 11, 1640) are in this same collection. In the former, the Archbishop thanks Sir William for his great care about the English church at Rotterdam and adds a postcript saying: "I heare from Mr. Le Maire That the States Generall are willing to sett out a Generall Proclamation over all the Provinces against Libellous Bookes, and particularly against those of Scotland, if you shall be pleased att anie tyme to signifie his Majesties Desire therein. If you can finde this to bee soe, I thinke you shall doe the King and the State acceptable service if you can gett it done, and the sooner the better."

which I presume are very harty and reall, and I pray be confident I shall be as ready to doe you all the Service I can as any other Friend you have in Court.

Mr. Secretary Cooke imparted unto me the Letters which you sent unto him, and I thank you very hartily for the care which by them I see you have taken for the Church. I hope his Majesty will not loose the opportunity which he now hath of settling conformity amongst the Merchants at Delft. And this assure yourself, Mr. Forbes shall never come thither againe, unlesse he will conforme himself in all things, which I knowe he will not doe, at least in that place. I pray have an Eye what becomes of Mr. Davenport and let me hear of it.

I have receyved the Booke you sent me, and I thank you for that alsoe, but I had one of them before, sent me by Vossius, whose Sonne I thinke translated it. If it be your happ to see Vossius, I pray commend me to him, and tell him, it is onely the multitude of my busyness that makes my Penne soe slowe, else he had heard from me before this tyme. Soe wishing you happy success in your affaires, I leave you to Gods grace and rest.

Your very lovinge Friend

W: Cant.

XVII.

Letter by Stephen Goffe to Sir William Boswell. Brussells, August 19/29, 1633.[38]

Worthy Sir,

This day ther hath come a new church business amongst us from Bergen-op-Zome, Wherein Mr. Paine, the minister which Mr. Forbes made out of my Lords company, hath troubled himselfe about our common prayers; one Capt. Clarke of Colonel Pagneheims regiment having the command of one of the Sconces neere the towne because neither himselfe nor his company could come to the church thought it best that one of his soldiers should read some prayers and chapters to

38 *Boswell Papers*, I, fol. 152. The address is still intact, with seal, and reads: "To the right Worshipfull my worthy friend Sir William Boswell, knight, Agent for His Majestie of Great Brittaine in the Hague—this."

them in the Sconce.   But this was so greivous to Mr. Paine
that he gott the Dutch ministers of the towne to goe with him
& joyne in the admonishing of Capt. Clarke, & forbidding
the thing to be done.   Which now the Captain complaines of
to his Colonel & his Colonel to General Morgan, their Governor,
who sweares he will never be troubled with these puritans &
as soone as he comes home will put him out.   I could wish the
business had happened on any rather then Capt. Clarke, who
hath beene a very Extreame Scandalous liver, yet now they
say he is repenting, & if so God forbid but he should have
liberty to pray.   The Businesse of the Busse stil hangs in
suspence, And there hath beene some art used more then honest
to have brought in Mr. Forbes his sonne, in that One went
to the Captaines as sent from my Lord Vere in his name to
require them to call him, when his Lordship was so far from
doing of it that he utterly misliked the man in some respects.
But whether Mr. Gribbins will goe or noe it is yet uncertaine;
and if he do this is wrought by him for One, & the old *Sticklers*
that the ministers of the Busse are all possessed against the
desire of the Captain in having our church orders observed,
insomuch that they have professed that they will Hinder any
man whoever shal come from doing of it.   This is the continual
practice of those men to draw the Dutch on their side & make
an outcry.   I see there is more trouble comming; for that the
officers do protest they wil not pay any man that wil not conforme, nor Mr. Gribbins himselfe though he do stay for his
good behaviour.   For the military newes since my last weekes
intelligence proved a litle to haply, because our supplies came
to us yesterday.   I wil forbeare till the event appeare.   And so
I rest

Your humble servant,
Stephen Goffe.

We shal shortly have great church news out of England upon
the great change.   Dr. Juxon you see according to my con-
jecture is a very likely to be the rising man.

The orders this night are for the soldier to victual himselfe for 5 daies.   And for the sailers for 14 daies.   The Prince
hath beene in councell with the States at Busse today, & hath
taken his leave of his Princesse.

XVIII.

Letter by Stephen Goffe to Sir William Boswell. Leiden, December 13/23, 1633.[39]

Sir,

Because of my many jornise I was willing not to have move out of Leyden this weeke, & so desired Mr. [Hugh] Goodyer to admitt me to the sacrament at his church. His answer was that he could do nothing without his Elders, & without publishing my name after his sermon to his congregation. I told him if that were but a matter of forme only, & That in his owne opinion he thought there would be no exception nor doubt that then I was contented. He said that he could not tell that, for he was affraid some of his parish would be scandalized att me. And when he made so many rubbs from his people, I desired him to Express himselfe in his owne Judgement; he said the time was too short to consider of so many particulars as in my case must be considered, as whether I were not a Nonresident or no, for that I ought not to live from my souldiers; Whether I did use to come to church, or no, for that I was not constantly at his church; And he had particular Exception against me for that halfe a year agoe in discourse with him I said that those men who had no imposition of hands neither from a Byshop nor by a Classicall autority could not be said to be ministers rightly called & ordained. And that he confessed he was such a one who had imposition of hands only by a french minister of this towne, & that by entreaty of his people, no classical authority sending him to do it. For the two former I gave sufficient answer, & for this last, because I never knew this of him, I said litle to it but only that he is reputed no minister, & by my presence at his sacrament if he would testifie my allowance of him for a minister, though were I in his case I should take more comfort

39 *Boswell Papers*, I, fol. 163. Endorsed verso: "Goffe 13/23 Dec. 1633. Leyden." Goffe wrote to William Brough from The Hague, Dec. 16/26, 1633: "Being at Leyden, I desired Mr. Goodyer, the minister there, to admitt me to the Sacrament. He did stoutly reject me for being a nonresident and a man that had a prejudice to such Ministers as he was. I thank God with all my heart for this, for I heare since this that he is no minister, so far from having ordination in England that he never had any ordination by any Classis, English nor Dutch neither. This is most certaine."—In *State Papers* 16, vol. 252, fol. 55 (Public Record Office, London). See also *Calendar of State Papers, Dom. Ser., Chas. I, 1633-34*, 324.

in it if I had beene lawfuly authorised; And so my earnest desire was that to morrow by noone he would resolve me. He told me he could not thinke of it now & that I must forbeare. I alledged for my selfe that Mr. Pagett did admitt me at Amsterdam but nothing would prevaile. My purpose ergo is to come to morrow to the Hage, but because I take it this is a matter of greater moment than that which particularly toucheth my person, I thought it my duty to give account of it unto Your selfe. And if any thing els be to be done, I beseech (as I have alwaies most happly hade) your counsell in it. For herein it is plaine my crime is that I am of the Faith of the church of England. I shall next weeke heare from Amsterdam. Mr. Pagett's cozen is gonne thither to returne next weeke. One of Mr. Davenport's frends was discoursing this day, that he thought he would not be chosen for that Mr. Pagett would be against him & that Mr. Davenport would not be of the Dutch Classis. I am sure nothing is done yet. Unlesse you can advise me better how to deal with this carefull pastor, I must come seeke another fold. In the meane time I rest

Your most thankful & devoted servant
of your other business I
wilbring account tomorrow. Stephen Goffe.

XIX.

Letter by John Tracy [or Trasy] to John Paget. Amsterdam, September 30, 1634.[40]

Reverend Mr. Paget, It grieveth me, that I have againe occasion to trouble you, whose days especially being now so Aged ought to be spent in peace & quietnes. Were it not for your Continued opposition of the truth & disgraceing the most deare servants of God, I should be very loath to doe any thing that might any way disquiet you. The Lord knowes how really I could love & imbrace you & reverence you more in divers regards, if you erred not so farre from the truth & so apparantly resist the power of religion, & them that would further the same.

If it were onely in one person or two, we might make some other construction of things, but not onely not to imbrace

---

40 In "Tracts Relating to the Dutch Church in Amsterdam . . . 1634." *Additional Manuscripts 24666*, fols. 17-19 (British Museum, London).

but to oppose so many eminent servants of God, cannot have any [other] Color. What an excellent man was that Mr. Parker; there are many will witness both here & in England especially, & yet you let him be here such a long time without once preaching; at Last when he preacht, & was desired of the church, you opposed him & kept him out.

How often have you opposed Mr. Pot both in publick teaching & many private vexations, the many Complaints that I have heard doth testify; though now you be kind to his wife & children, & divers others, by hospitality, Gifts, & Lending of money; some whome you have beene so kind unto of late wonder at it, seing you have not invited them so many yeares before; but though you may deceive simple People & Children by your liberality, yet others see herein a factious disposition to make a party; & yet some to speake well of you, especially you labour to get such on your side which are great talkers, & free of speech, or such as goe much abroad to other folks houses to worke, that thereby they might speake of you well to many; & give you intelligence from every house what they here & see. But to get such on your side as are most forward for religion that you looke not after.

When Mr. Peter was desired to be here, how did you so worke the busines that Mr. Pot seemed most to oppose it & you would not be seene in the business. But as I heard the good man said, it wilbe knowne hereafter whither I or Mr. Paget did most oppose Mr. Peter, as hath well appeared since.

What an eminent servant of God was Mr. Hooker, both for gifts & godliness? Yet him you opposed also, & kept him out in spight of the whole Eldership & Church; When Mr. Ames, & Mr. Forbes were nominated to be here, them you opposed also; & yet where are there more eminent men then these, & such as have suffred much for the very same Cause, for which you left the Church of England, every one of them; & Lastly, how basely have you opposed Mr. Davenport we all with grief of heart have taken knowledge, & as some of your Cheife members said, if Mr. Paget had not dissembled with us, he had never depreived us of him; but when he came over, O you were so glad of it, & that God had sent him in a need-full time, & in the highest degree of love & protestation seemed to desire him before any man; but it hath well appeared how you desired him.

For, First, when the Elders & people urged often to the finishing of the Election, you all ways opposed & deferred it; & also so often murmured against him because he came over without your sending for. I warrant you, he might have stayed long enough before you would have sent for him, or any other eminent man. Also you did almost plainly preach against him before he came & disgraced him, as if he had Cowardly Cast downe the Standard & left his place unlawfully; which when you heare the particular relation of afterward from himself, you justifyed every particular, & Commended much his wisdome & Care therin. Againe, as soone as you found his Judgement to differ in this poynt of Baptisms, from yours, then you thought you had enough; & as I said before to some, you shall see Mr. Paget will never leave talking with Mr. D. Till he may find some difference of Judgment, & then he will say yes I love & desire the man, & I desire we might have him, but for his error; & Just so it fell out. For I saw before you dissembled in your great profession of love; though they which were angry with me, & beleeved it not at first, could say it was too true afterwards when you had once found a difference. You refused all wayes of accomodation. Mr. D. offred to beare with your both Judgment & practice in baptiseing all, & desired that you would but do the like with him. No, by no means, you said it would make a breach in the Church; then he tould you it might be hidden, & none of the Church need to know you differed therein, & that either you might baptise those he would not, or let them go to the dutch Church; but you would doe neither of both, though he offered you to baptise the Children of all members, onely those out of the Church he desired he might first know what they were. Then you had many private disputes about the poynt, but noe Arguments You would yeild unto, though never so plainly Gods will; till at last you refused to dispute any more with him, though now you untruly report he refused to dispute with you; whereas I heard himself say there passed two or three serious disputes betweene you, which he hath in writeing by him, & that he never ceased till you gave over, & said, seing your Judgment Could not prevaile with him, you would now leave it to the

dutch ministers, to see if they Can prevaile with him: from
which though he persuaded you earnestly by divers reasons,
saying it would make the difference the greater &c, yet you
would not be persuaded (for to make the difference greater
was your desire), but at last tould him, you would no more
speake with him alone about those matters, & therefore Mr.
Davenport Ceased disputing with you. & for the dutch
ministers, when Mr. D. would reason the poynt, they answered
they came not to dispute, & therefore Cease such slanders; &
to say he refused to dispute.   At last when the Elders, deacons,
& members & noe intreatys would prevaile with you, you said
you would bring it to the Classis (though against their mindes)
& in the meane time you got five of the duch ministers into
your house, & there got them to make a writeing under their
hands, in which, without any argument, you would have Mr.
D. rest; & this was the dispute you procured from the dutch:
The upper part of the letter one might see was their doeing,
wherein they Commended Mr. D. Care for the Purity of the
Ordinance, & desired it might be done according to his mind
as farre as it might stand with the edification of the english
Church; by which they enough gave to understand their
minds; as afterward divers of them privately desired it might
be privately made an end of amongst you, & oft spake with
some Elders & others, saying, why cannot this be made an
end of amongst yourselvs; & whereas you now give out & still
make shew, as if you would have had Mr. D. if the Classis
would have suffred it; who sees not the contrary, that know
anything of this busines.   The Classes would faine have past
it over, if you would; which divers of them manifested by
their great desire not to have it Come at the Classes, & when
it came there no man opposed his acceptance, though so many
of them knew the difference, & Commanded you to give him
a Be-roepbrief, though you opposed it; till afterward you
brought it by force to the Classes againe & urged them to make
an order about it.   In which you knew they would raither
oppose Mr. D. then make a publick act to condemne their owne
practice.   O, Mr. Paget all those subtle tricks will not helpe
you when God comes to awaken your Conscience.   And the
duch ministers themselves, unlesse 2 or 3, are not well Content
with your doings; though they would not make a publick act

against themselves, which you would have or els keepe out
Mr. Davenport. For many of them privately shake their
heads at your doeings; & as some of the Cheife of them desired
one of the Elders but to keepe Mr. D. from haveing too much
conference with you, & then you should not keepe out Mr. D.
as you did Mr. Hooker. So who knowes not that many, both
duch & English ministers in the Land, though of sundry
Classes, will not baptise all that are brought without any
exception, as you urged Mr. D. You yourself, as I heare,
sent back divers this yeare that were brought you to baptise:
& that long since you would not baptise all, & in particular
refused the Child of Jo: Sp: which what all these things
testify, but that you strained your Conscience to keepe out
Mr. D. I know not.

Yea, There are Divers of their owne Synods have made
expresse order against baptiseing of all presented without any
exception; & your self was content to have Mr. Bamfords in
the haeg, though he expresly denyed you to baptise all, which
my selfe & divers others heard him testify, & though your
self denye it. Yet have you since that time, named divers,
to be such as you nominated to be ministers here, though you
know they will not baptise all Children. So that for my part,
I cannot but beleeve, that as Saull could not indure the presence of David, for his eminency, so Cannot your Spirit indure
any minister in this Church more eminent then your selfe;
which others see as well as I, & how all your plots tend to
have a man of meaner gifts; but be sure the Lord will find
you out; & it may be by your own plots, make you see your
evill herein, in which so long as you Continue unrepentant.
Pardon me, though I make thus bould with you, & oppose your
doeings for the truths sake. I know I shall expose my selfe
to your Pulpit bitternes, but know that I regard not your
self preaching, & unjust reproches; it may be also you will
by subtill insinuations stir up some others to reproch me, but
I hope the Lord will inable me to beare all your bitternes,
who is greater than all.

For my part I beare you no ill will, but truly desire your
everlasting good, & therefore have taken so much paines to
discover unto you, your miscariages if it were possible. I
pray you take the pains to peruse this Answer to your Argu-

ment for baptiseing all presented without exception, it may bee the Lord may yet open your eyes to see the truth. I have not bound my self precisely to your words, because I would take away exceptions, but laid downe the substance of your Arguments with the answer thereunto; smaller matters I pray you passe by in me, who want both time & ability to peruse, & digest my first thoughts. And so leaving you to the mercifull God who is yet able to doe wonderfully for you above all our expectations I rest.

Yours
John Trasy.

XX.

Extracts from a Letter by J. C. Flexham to Sir William Boswell. Delft, February 26, 1636, n.s.[41]

[Flexham recently visited at Delft his cousin, the Reverend Mr. Spranckhuysens, who told of the] Publick Scandall and rayling sermon which Patrick Forbes made to his audience upon Sunday morning the 17th of February, 1636, Stilo Novo. [The church council at Delft assembled yesterday] to inform themselves thereof from some of the English Congregation . . . and as soone as they have gott there depositions will send that to you by my selfe, to take your advise upon it.

Now for the opening of the Gesthouse Church unto them, he tould mee that he was informed that upon the selicitation of these English men abovenamed [Messrs. Focts, Turvill, Eaton, & Brockes] and some others, having promised the magistrates of Delfe that they would procure a preacher and diverse families, Tradesmen, to come out of England to dwell in this towne, the magistrates upon this hope had given them this church provisionally, and that they might preach in that; . . . and with all, one of their Burgomasters was deputed to solicite the States of Holland for a Competence and meanes to maintayne their preacher as other Townes of Holland have; but this the magistrate did without the advise and knowledge of the Kerkenradt, which is against order and not well relished. Neither doe the Kerckenradt know by whom or from whome Patrick Forbes had his ordination to be a

41 *Boswell Papers*, I, fol. 219.

preacher. Till this information be gotten, he beseeches you to have patience, and as soone as they have it they will send it unto you and take your advise what is best to be done in it. For he tells me the Kerckenradt in Delfe are resolved that they must either conforme themselves to the orders of the Church of England or, at Least, to the Netherlandish Church where they live, and observe sett formes of prayers, as also in administering of Baptisme & the Lords Supper. For the English Liturgie he hath a reverend opinion of it, hath read the booke of Common prayer, and besides, hath examined it by Doctour Bois his booke which he showed mee, and finds it Conformable to Gods Word and doth protest that if he were Minister in the Dutch Church in London, if the King or the Archbishop of Canterbury should enjoyne him to read it, he would make noe scruples to doe it with a good Conscience to that Auditorie.

INDEX

Abbot, Dr. George, Archbishop, 18, 19, 77.

Amarant, Paul, Utrecht minister, 93-95.

Amboyna dispute, 31.

Ames, Dr. William, on Congregational polity, 4-7; chaplain to Lord Vere, 12 *n*; member of classis, 15; to teach in new Congregational college at Rotterdam, 54; his *Fresh Suit Against Ceremonies*, 29 *n*, 57, 118; intended to go to New England, 71; death of, 71; his "Cases of Conscience," 109-11; mentioned, 3, 23, 30, 50, 55, 68, 75 *n*, 142.

"Amesians," 3.

Amsterdam, Dutch classis of, considers Hooker's fitness, 28-29, 116; considers Davenport's fitness, 64-68, 141, 144; fears English classis, 69, 115; mentioned, 61, 114.

Anglican (-s), 2, 4, 7, 16, 21, 29. (*See also* England, Church of.)

Antholins, St., Collectors of, 21-22.

Arminianism, 19, 20, 26, 83, 103.

Avery, Samuel, replaces Misselden at Delft, 43; discharged, 48; mentioned, 33.

Bachelor, Samuel, of Gorinchem, member of English classis, 15, 66, 87; opposes Book of Common Prayer, 44, 48-51, 74, 133-34; mentioned, 84, 86, 91, 114.

Balmford, Samuel, of The Hague, member of English classis, 15, 87; called before the Dutch Council, 52, 134; goes to England, 71; called to Amsterdam, 116; mentioned, 51, 86, 135, 145.

Bancroft, Richard, Archbishop, 18.

Baptists, 2.

Barkeley, Thomas, of Rotterdam, 15, 84, 89.

Baxter, Richard, 76.

Baynes, Paul, 60, 110, 115.

Beaumont, George, succeeds Forbes at Delft, 48; leaves Delft, 73.

Bladwell, Richard, replaces Avery as Delft Deputy, 48.

"Boswell Papers," account of, 77-79.

Boswell, Sir William, English Ambassador to The Hague, sketch of, 77-79; supports Misselden against Forbes, 41-42, 45-47; efforts to dissolve English classis, 43, 45, 52-69, 114, 123-24; enforces conformity among English chaplains, 45, 49, 51-53; dispatch to Secretary Coke, 131-35; mentioned, 35, 36, 136, 138, 140, 146.

Bridge, William, at Rotterdam, 74.

Bridges, Francis, 21 *n*.

Brown, Alexander, informer for Boswell, 43, 55, 56, 57.

Brown, Samuel, 21 *n*.

"Brownists," 4, 29, 60, 61, 105, 106, 115, 117.

Burroughs, Jeremiah, at Rotterdam, 74.

Buttler, Ephraim, of Utrecht, 88.

Calvinism, 4.

Carleton, Sir Dudley, Viscount Dorchester, English Ambassador to The Hague, disciplines English classis, 9, 11, 23-24; on early supervision of English churches in Holland, 13 *n*; recall of, 27; assists in organization of Utrecht English church, 88; articles to the English and Scottish ministers, delivered by, 95-96; mentioned, 41, 78, 97, 135.

Cavalier, 3.

Cecill, General, 90.

Charles I, order to Merchant Adventurers, 46; letter by (extract), 104-105; mentioned, 18, 19, 20, 23, 62, 75, 78.

Charles II, 44 *n*.

Clarke, Alexander, 15, 84? 87?

Clarke, George, 15, 84? 87?

Classis, Congregational functions of, 5-6.

Classis, English Congregational in the Dutch Netherlands, organization of, 8-11, 114; James I's grant for, 9; Dutch States aproval of, 10-11; membership of, 14-16, 114; assumes powers unintended by English king, 23-24, 55-59, 114-15; reply to English Privy Council (1628), 24-26, 97-104; Sir Henry Vane's instructions to, 27; supports Hooker for the Amsterdam church, 28-29; differs from English and Dutch Reformed church-